Other titles in the series

LATE-BREAKING
AMAZING STORIES™

TERRORISM
THE HOMELAND THREAT
The truth behind the everpresent danger

T 34828

by Stan Sauerwein

Altitude Publishing

PUBLISHED BY ALTITUDE PUBLISHING LTD.
1500 Railway Avenue, Canmore, Alberta T1W 1P6
www.amazingstoriesbooks.com
1-800-957-6888

Extreme care has been taken to ensure that the information contained in this book is accurate and up to date at the time of printing. However, neither the author nor the publisher is responsible for errors, omissions, loss of income or anything else that may result from the information contained in this book.

Publisher	Stephen Hutchings
Associate Publisher	Kara Turner
Canadian Editor	Heather Hudak
U.S. Editor	Julian S. Martin
Fact Checker	Andy Sayers
Maps and tables	Scott Dutton

We acknowledge the financial support of the Government of Canada through the Book Publishing Industry Development Program (BPIDP) for our publishing activities.

ALTITUDE GREENTREE PROGRAM
Altitude Publishing will plant twice as many trees as were used in the manufacturing of this product.

In order to make this book as universal as possible, all currency is shown in US dollars.

Cataloging in Publication Data
Sauerwein, Stan, 1952-
    Terrorism : the homeland threat / Stan Sauerwein.

(Late breaking amazing stories)
ISBN 1-55265-303-X (American mass market edition)
ISBN 1-55439-501-1 (Canadian mass market edition)

    1. Terrorism--North America. I. Title. II. Series.

HV6433.N67S29 2005   303.6'25   C2005-905269-4

In Canada, Amazing Stories® is a registered trademark of Altitude Publishing Canada Ltd. An application for the same trademark is pending in the U.S.

Printed and bound in Canada by Friesens
2 4 6 8 9 7 5 3 1

"America will never seek a permission slip to defend the security of our people."

President George W. Bush

CONTENTS

The U.S. Customs agents responsible for capturing
terrorist Ahmed Ressam in 1999. From left: Dan Clem,
Mark Johnson, Diane Dean, and Mike Chapman.
The inscription, top right, was written by former
Commissioner of U.S. Customs Ray Kelly and reads
"Thanks for what you did for America." (For more on
the capture of Ahmed Ressam, see page 25.)

Osama bin Laden, left, with his top lieutenant,
Egyptian Ayman al-Zawahri, in an Al-Jazeera television
broadcast in October 2001. (For more on bin
Laden and al-Zawahri, see pages 83 and 104.)

Peter Clarke, head of Britain's Metropolitan Police
Service's Anti-Terrorist branch, holds up a food container similar to the type used by the men linked to
the July 21, 2005, attempted London bombings. The
plastic food containers were used to hold the bombs
and were concealed in rucksacks. (For more
on the London terrorists, see page 43.)

British prime minister Tony Blair (left) greets U.S.
President George W. Bush during the Group of Eight
summit in Scotland, July 7, 2005. A series of bombs
rocked London, England, the same day. (For more
on the London bombings, see page 30.)

Islamic fundamentalist cleric Ayatollah Ruhollah
Khomeini, center, waves to followers as he appears
on the balcony of his headquarters in Tehran, Iran,
in February 1979 on return from exile. (For more
on the Ayatollah, see page 79.)

Little remains of the bombed Rut Para al-Qaeda training camp west of Kandahar, Afghanistan, January
2002. American and local anti-Taliban forces raided
the camp, collecting evidence from its bunkers and
mountain caves. (For more on al-Qaeda
training camps, see page 100.)

CHAPTER 1

Introducing Ahmed Ressam—Terrorist Wannabe

The glory of killing Americans when the world celebrated the new millennium was all the 32-year-old Algerian national thought about for nearly a year. He scouted the death site, recruited zealot accomplices, and meticulously prepared his murder weapons. As the deadline to mayhem approached, Ressam thought he'd devised a foolproof plan, but he hadn't realized something very simple: U.S.

Customs officers on the border between Canada and the United States do not accept Costco membership cards as picture identification.

Like an unknown number of his extremist brethren, Ressam was among a massive population of illegal residents living among North Americans. Three years earlier, the U.S. Immigration and Naturalization Service (INS) estimated five million illegal residents were hiding in the United States. Between 1981 and 1991, Canada admitted 279,000 people as permanent residents on humanitarian grounds. By the time Ressam moved to Canada, the country had more than 100,000 deportation orders on the books with a backlog that grew by 10 percent a year. Canadian and U.S. immigration officials did not know how many legal or illegal immigrants lived in their respective countries. They also did not know if any might attempt acts of terror.

Growing Up in Algeria
Ressam was born in Algeria in 1967, just five

years after the French lowered the last Tricolor and pulled out of the African colony. When the Islamic Front for Salvation (FIS) gained control of Algeria in the early 1990s, Ressam decided to flee. He grew up in a household familiar with western culture, and although it contradicted his Muslim upbringing, he embraced it. The FIS opposed American cultural ideals. They professed leadership according to the *shariah*, laws derived from strict interpretations of the Koran. Ressam had a penchant for western designer clothes and a lifestyle filled with nightclubbing and alcohol consumption. Under the FIS, these habits branded him a criminal.

Fleeing to North America

On September 5, 1992, Ressam fled Algeria for Marseille, France, traveling on a 30-day visitor's visa. As an illegal immigrant, he managed to procure a false French passport and an airline ticket to Montreal, Canada. Holding the doctored passport, he applied for political asylum.

An immigration hearing was set to review his case the following March. In the meantime, Ressam received monthly welfare subsistence of $550. When he failed to appear for his hearing, authorities arrested and fingerprinted Ressam, and gave him a chance to appear on another court date.

To supplement his welfare payments, Ressam shoplifted and stole purses and suitcases. He wanted to stay in Canada but didn't know how to navigate the Canadian immigration system. Ressam turned to earlier Algerian immigrants. The Masjid as-Salam mosque in Montreal was a perfect place to meet such individuals. Here, he met Fateh Kamel, an Algerian who married a Canadian. Kamel became one of Ressam's advisors. Ressam's skill as a thief interested Kamel.

Several years earlier, French intelligence officers uncovered Kamel's name in the records of an Islamic terrorist, who had suspected links to al-Qaeda. At the time, 35-year-old Kamel fought as a *mujahideen* in Afghanistan and Bosnia and manufactured false documents for Islamic terrorists. He offered to pay Ressam for the passports or identity papers he found in stolen purses and suitcases. Ressam welcomed the job opportunity and managed to deliver documents at least 40 times before he was caught as a pickpocket in October 1996. Despite being an illegal immigrant with four previous convictions for thievery, including shoplifting, the sentencing judge gave Ressam a small

DEFINITION OF TERMS

mujahideen: The Arabic word means literally "person who wages *jihad*" or "holy warrior," but the term is more commonly used to denote Muslim armed fighters.
jihad: A holy war, or "struggle" waged on behalf of Islam as a religious duty

For more definitions see the Glossary on page 172–173.

fine, put him on probation for two years, and then released him from custody.

Ressam's work for Kamel gave him some notoriety among Algerian expatriates. Through these associations, he met Abderraouf Hannachi. Hannachi, in his mid-40s, was a regular at the Assuna Annabawiyah mosque, where he openly criticized what he saw as the West's decadent culture. He called western dress immoral; its music godless. From the safety of the mosque, Hannachi worked tirelessly to attract young Muslims like Ressam, encouraging them to join the holy war against the United States.

Hannachi told young Muslim men that he trained at one of Osama bin Laden's camps in Afghanistan. At the Khalden camp, Hannachi learned how to fire handguns, assault rifles, and grenade launchers. He was well versed in the secrets of urban warfare, too, and other young Muslims also could learn these secrets. He implored young Muslims to heed the call of leaders in the global *jihad.*

Ressam had not come to Canada to become a terrorist. However, Kamel and Hannachi enthralled Ressam and his friends with their stories of the jihad. At 6301 Place de la Malicorne, an apartment Ressam shared with friends, the men planned their own excursions to partici-

DELAYED ACTION: THE CASE OF MOHAMMAD YOUSSEF HAMMOUD

Lebanese Shiite Muslim Mohammad Youssef Hammoud first entered the United States on June 6, 1992, aged 18 years, with a fake U.S. visa. Authorities caught him immediately but allowed Hammoud to enter the country pending an investigation of his status. Five months later, Hammoud requested political asylum. Another 13 months passed before a judge refused his request. Hammoud appealed the deportation order, and a year later, in December 1994, married an American. Eighteen months later, the Immigration and Naturalization Service (INS) determined the marriage was a fake. Again, a judge ordered Hammoud be deported in a month's time. Still, Hammoud remained in the U.S., and the INS did little to enforce the deportation order. In May 1997, Hammoud married again, and in September, he married a third time without first divorcing his second wife. Poor record keeping failed to track him. Hammoud received a green card in July 1998. He was finally caught in 2003 by a joint task force, and tried, convicted, and sentenced to 155 years in prison for aiding the terror group *Hezbollah*.

pate in the jihad. They did not realize authorities recorded their conversations.

French authorities alerted the Canadian

Security Intelligence Service (CSIS) to Kamel's connections with Islamic terrorists. Placing Kamel under surveillance led the CSIS to Ressam and his friends, a group the French eagerly called a terrorist "cell." The CSIS, however, saw no real danger in the men's idle boasting about jihad. In fact, the CSIS operatives who listened to the conversations called the apartment "BOG"—short for "Bunch of Guys"—and classed the meetings as little more than terrorist Tupperware parties. Over time, the CSIS compiled a 400-page dossier on BOG, but they didn't share the information with other authorities. The CSIS were assigned to protect national security, and BOG's conversations did not threaten security. What the CSIS didn't know was that Hannachi was a successful al-Qaeda recruiter. He worked closely with Abu Zubaydah, who coordinated the entry of al-Qaeda recruits to Afghanistan.

Hannachi told Zubaydah he had a good recruit with a fresh identity. To avoid immigration,

Ressam stole a blank baptismal certificate from a Catholic church, picked himself a new birthday and a new name—Benni Antoine Noris—and obtained a legitimate Canadian passport.

Terrorist in Training

On March 16, 1998, Ressam began his journey to Afghanistan. Zubaydah met Ressam in Peshawar, Pakistan. He outfitted the young man and sent him, along with other raw recruits, over the Khyber Pass to Osama bin Laden's Khalden camp in Afghanistan. The Khalden camp was a small area consisting of four tents and four stone buildings. As many as 100 recruits at a time, grouped by nationality, received their initial terrorist training. By September, Ressam graduated and moved to another camp, where he learned bomb-making skills.

In mid-January 1999, Ressam transformed from a petty thief into a terrorist, willing to sacrifice himself for jihad. His first assignment was to return to North America, buy passports and weapons, and build a bomb to destroy a target of his choice in the United States at the dawn of the new millennium. Passing through Los Angeles, Ressam decided one of the world's busiest airports, Los Angeles International Airport, was his target.

Once he returned to Montreal, Ressam went to work. He found two young Montreal men who had not been trained by al-Qaeda but wanted to join the jihad: an old friend, Abdel Majid Dahoumane, and a credit-card thief named Mokhtar Haouari. Ressam learned of another man from New York, a con man named Abdelghani Meskini, who never met Ressam in person. They agreed that Haouari would provide money for the operation, Dahoumane would help Ressam make his bomb, and Meskini would help deliver it to the target.

Preparing for the New Millennium

Ressam purchased supplies at electronics stores, and on November 17, 1999, he and

Dahoumane flew to Vancouver, British Columbia, to build the bomb. The two men brewed an explosive cocktail—Hexamethylene Triperoxide Diamine (HMTD)—from hexamine, citric acid, and hydrogen peroxide.

With the HMTD, Ressam planned to make a military-grade explosive called C4 plastique. After building the explosive, Dahoumane returned to Montreal, and Ressam began the first leg of his bombing mission from Vancouver to Seattle, Washington. On December 14, 1999, Ressam drove a rented car onto the Port Angeles ferry from Victoria, British Columbia. Arriving in Port Angeles at suppertime that evening, his was the last car to roll off the ferry.

Fortunately for travelers at the Los Angeles airport, U.S. Customs inspector Diana Dean was just as vigilant with the last car she inspected at the Port Angeles ferry dock as she was with her first. She noticed the driver appeared visibly feverish. He gave clipped and poorly pronounced one-word answers to her routine questions. To her honed instincts, the man was "hinky." Dean ordered the man to complete a Customs declaration, and when he finished, to get out of his car so she could inspect his trunk. Ressam did so reluctantly.

Other Customs officers, by that time finished with their own traffic lanes, moved over to help Dean process the last vehicle of the day. Dean told the officers she had a hunch this might be a "load vehicle," which was inspectors' code for a car or truck used to smuggle drugs. Inspector Mark Johnson stepped forward and addressed the driver in Spanish. Ressam replied in French and offered identification—his Costco membership card. This was peculiar behavior, and now Johnson was wary, as well. He asked Ressam to empty his pockets, while other inspectors checked the man's suitcase and the trunk of his car. It took only a few seconds for Inspector Danny Clem to call the other officers to the rear of Ressam's vehicle. Inside the trunk's spare-tire compartment, Clem uncovered several green bags filled with a white powder, four black boxes, two pill bottles and two jars of a brown liquid. The inspectors thought Ressam was a drug smuggler.

"Based on this discovery," Dean later reported, "an immediate pat down of Ressam was conducted, during which Ressam managed to slip out of his jacket and flee on foot."

Johnson and Inspector Mike Chapman ran after Ressam. Five blocks away, they spotted him crouching on the ground behind a parked car. They attempted to capture him, but Ressam bolted. In an intersection, he tried to commandeer a passing car but was unsuccessful, and the inspectors managed their arrest. Once they subdued him, they put Ressam in the custody of Port Angeles police. Soon, the Customs inspectors learned Ressam was not a drug smuggler. Instead, Dean tripped over four timing devices, 118 pounds (54 kg) of urea crystals, 14 pounds (6 kg) of RDX and HMDT in white powder form, and 3 pounds (1.4 kg) of EDGN—a gooey, brown, liquid-like nitroglycerin.

Ressam didn't stand trial until March 13, 2001. After a three-week hearing, a jury found him guilty of nine criminal counts, including conspiracy to commit an act of international terrorism. Under questioning, Ressam revealed terrifying facts about al-Qaeda.

CHAPTER 2

Under Attack

As the leaders of the world's most prosperous nations sat down to a private breakfast in Gleneagles, Scotland, on July 7, 2005, they prepared to discuss global climate change. The meal was the first event for the Group of Eight (G8) Summit that day.

At the same time, three million commuters started their work day, traveling along London's 250 miles (400 km) of subway. One day earlier, thousands took to the streets to celebrate that their city was chosen as the site of the 2012 Summer Olympics. In one of the most densely populated cities in Europe, everything seemed normal. However, at the height of the morning rush hour, normalcy changed to chaos. The rapid-fire events that suddenly gripped London were a hauntingly familiar echo of the same terrified confusion New Yorkers experienced during a morning rush hour nearly four years earlier.

At 8:50 a.m., British transport police received a report of an "incident" on the Metropolitan Line between Liverpool Street and the Aldgate East subway station. The incident was an explosion that tore through the train's third subway carriage, deep underground. The explosion instantly stole the lives of seven innocent commuters and simultaneously injured hundreds of others. The pieces of the victims' bodies—their clothes ripped away by the concussive force of the blast—suddenly scattered across the subway tracks. The explosion scorched survivors in the targeted carriage and in other carriages nearby the blast. Hair singed away and faces seared, they smashed through the carriage window glass with bare fists, in a panicked attempt to let fresh air into the smoke-filled subway cars.

Initially, officials on the surface streets of north London thought there was a power surge. They did not know a concerted terrorist attack gripped the city. Simultaneous to the first, two other bombs exploded. The second ripped through the first subway car on a train located between Russell Square and King's Cross stations. Another 21 innocents died instantly. The third bomb exploded at Edgware Road station, smashing a hole through the train's second car and the subway tunnel. The blast damaged three trains in all and claimed seven victims.

Just as the shock of those attacks sank in, at 9:47 a.m., the top of a double-decker bus exploded only a few steps from the British

Medical Association headquarters near Tavistock Square in central London, instantly killing 13 people plus the bomber. Immediately, a team of 14 doctors arrived on scene to treat casualties in a make-shift courtyard hospital.

Reuters news service quoted Dominic Armstrong, head of research and intelligence for Aegis Defense Services, with a likely explanation for a discrepancy in the pattern of attacks. "The most logical explanation is that one of the terrorists was unable to board an underground train—probably because of the rapid closure of the system—and ended up with a primed bomb and no target," he said.

Londoners, who had not witnessed such savagery since the Irish Republican Army (IRA) bombings in the 1980s and 1990s, scattered throughout the streets in shock. This was the worst attack on London since the Nazi Blitz of World War II.

Scott Wenbourne, a commuter on the train traveling into Aldgate station, witnessed the

Map showing the London bombings

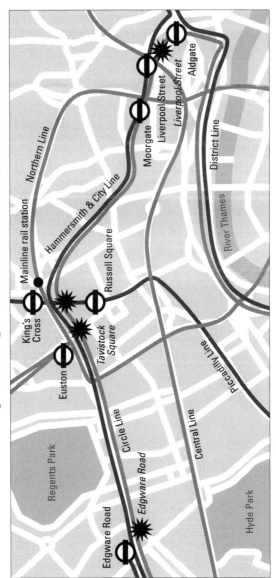

34828

Φ Underground   **✳** Bombing

explosion in the carriage ahead of him. The British Broadcasting Corporation (BBC) reported his grisly experience to the world, once rescuers managed to reach the twisted train wreckage.

"As we walked up past the carriage, we saw debris and torn metal. I noticed the carriage was completely ripped apart on one side. I saw three bodies on the track. I couldn't look, it was so horrific. I think one was moving but I'm not too sure."

During the hours that followed the four attacks, emergency vehicles and commandeered city buses moved 700 injured to six different London hospitals. Curbside triage sorted the walking wounded from the dying, as the media learned of a climbing death toll. By the evening commute, officials reported the body count had reached 38. Forty-five victims were described as seriously injured.

British prime minister, Tony Blair, rushed to calm and reassure his nation after the bombings, flanked in support by the leaders of the other G8 nations. Terrorists will not succeed in destroying "our values and our way of life," Prime Minister Blair said. "It is particularly barbaric this had happened on a day when people are meeting to try to help the problems of poverty in Africa. It is important that those engaged in terrorism realize that our determination to defend our values and our way of life is greater than their determination to cause death and destruction to innocent people in a desire to impose extremism on the world."

Investigating the Attacks

By Friday morning, the grim-faced London Metropolitan Police commissioner, Sir Ian Blair, had no progress to report on the hunt for the perpetrators. The death toll had climbed to at least 49. Fearing the blast between King's Cross and Russell Square made the tunnel unstable, rescuers left about 25 victims' bodies in the rubble overnight. However, Blair assured the country, "the entire weight of the antiterrorism branch of Scotland Yard is aimed implacably at the investigation." By July 18, the death toll rose to 56, including the bombers.

After examining forensic evidence found at the scenes of the explosions, Andy Hayman, head of the police's antiterrorist branch, said each of the four bombs contained less than 10 pounds (4.5 kg) of high explosives. Explosives experts claimed the bombers likely used simple, relatively easy-to-obtain plastic explosives. If they had used higher-grade military plastics, such as Semtex, the devastation would have been much worse, they said.

Investigators began reviewing 40,000 hours of closed-circuit television (CCTV) footage, captured by more than 6,000 cameras monitoring the London Underground. Britain became a world leader in surveillance when they began using such cameras to fight IRA bombers in London in 1992 and 1993. Police hoped they might catch a glimpse of the perpetrators in action. By July 11, police said they viewed grainy

CCTV footage of four bomber suspects together in King's Cross station at 8:30 a.m., about 20 minutes before the blasts. Ian Blair said forensic evidence found at the attack scenes, including some of the dead men's belongings, indicated the men were Britain's first suicide bombers. He also announced that at least three British-born men likely carried out the bombings. They arrested a relative of one of the suspects for questioning.

Additional details emerged after authorities carried out intelligence-led raids on six homes in Leeds. According to newspaper reports, the raids uncovered explosives. Some speculated the bombers drove a rental car to Luton, 30 miles (50 km) north of London, and then boarded a commuter train to London's King Cross station.

Police identified four suspects who died in the bombings. They were 22-year-old Shehzad Tansweer, who likely caused the blast between Liverpool Street and Aldgate stations; 18-year-old Hasib Mir Hussain 18, who possibly caused the

Tavistock explosion; Mohammed Sidique Khan, 30, of Dewsbury, West Yorkshire, who allegedly blew up the Edgware Road train; and Germaine Morris Lindsay, a 19-year-old Jamaican-born man whose mother lived in the United States. Lindsay lived 40 miles (65 km) northwest of London. Police raided his house in Aylesbury on July 13.

The Metropolitan Police also focused their hunt on Magdy el-Nashar, 33, an Egyptian chemistry student who disappeared from his house in Leeds, and on a mysterious sixth suspect, who entered the country two weeks before the attacks. The sixth suspect was listed on an antiterrorist watch list, but British officials did not consider him a threat to national security or a high priority for surveillance. According to press reports that emerged during the early stages of the investigation, the man reportedly left Britain shortly before the bombers struck, which raised police suspicions.

Searching for the Suspects

El-Nashar was a biochemist who attended Leeds University after studying chemical engineering at North Carolina State University in Raleigh. In October 2000, the National Research Center in Cairo sponsored el-Nashar's doctoral studies on environmentally friendly "chemically inactive substances" with implications for the food industry. He earned his doctorate in Leeds on May 6.

On July 15, 2005, authorities arrested el-Nashar at the Cairo International Airport and held him for questioning. Under Egypt's 24-year-old Emergency Law, authorities can detain suspects for months without charges. El-Nashar's alleged link to the plot was unclear. Officials believed he gave the bombers keys to a house in Leeds—the same house at which police uncovered a cache of explosive substances in the bathtub during raids that took place days after the blasts. They found a highly volatile substance, triacetone triperoxide (TATP), which

POSSIBLE TERRORISM TARGETS: TRANSPORTATION

Statistics on 22,237 terrorism incidents since 1968 gathered by the Oklahoma City-based Memorial Institute for the Prevention of Terrorism showed transportation ranked in the top five preferred targets for terrorist attacks. In a normal rush hour at New York's Penn Station, more than 1,600 people flow in and out each minute. In Chicago, riders take more than 1.5 million trips on the city's elevated railway each day. Every year, the Washington, D.C., Metrorail subway handles more than 200 million trips. In total, on an average day, 14 million Americans use public buses, trains, and subways. Because security has increased on airplanes, some experts warn that terrorists may switch to "softer" targets of mass transit.

they believed was the same substance British "shoe bomber," Richard Reid, used during an attempt to blow up a commercial airline flight from Paris, France, to Miami, Florida, in 2001. In 2003, a U.S. court convicted Reid and sentenced him to life in prison. El-Nashar's telephone number appeared on a cell phone that was recovered in the investigation, as well. However, during questioning, el-Nashar denied any involvement in the bombings, and Egyptian authorities agreed, refusing the British request to extradite their suspect.

The BBC cited sources close to the investigation that appeared to contradict El-Nashar's alibi. Neighbors told police that El-Nashar claimed he left Britain because of a visa problem. After his arrest, the suspect stated he traveled to Egypt on a vacation two weeks earlier. Upon arrival in Egypt, El-Nashar delivered his Ph.D. thesis to the National Research Center's chemistry department and a week later told colleagues that he was going on a 45-day vacation.

Intelligence reports on all of the suspects began to emerge from other parts of the world, as well. Pakistani security agents claimed that three of the accused suicide bombers visited Pakistan in 2004. Hasib Hussain flew to Pakistan a year before the London bombings. Mohammad Sidique Khan and Shehzad Tanweer arrived and left together after spending three months in that country. In 2003, Tanweer met with a man who was later arrested for bombing a church in the Pakistani capital of Islamabad. Pakistan security agents investigated Tanweer's possible links with militant groups based in their country.

Ian Blair told the BBC that detectives on the case were confident they would find an al-Qaeda link to the British bombings. Claims of responsibility supported this contention. British foreign secretary, Jack Straw, said the attacks bore all the hallmarks of the al-Qaeda network; however, terrorism experts debated. Security authorities carefully argued about the identity of those responsible. Was it a homegrown group? Did a bomb expert, perhaps a survivor of al-Qaeda in Afghanistan or Pakistan, come to London to teach the British group how to make bombs?

"From the terrorists' point of view," news services quoted Straw as saying, "it seems they [al-Qaeda] have calculated they need to do just one significant terrorist attack a year in another capital, and it regenerates the same fear and anxieties."

Exactly two weeks after the Underground blasts killed 56 people, London was thrown into chaos again. Despite the fact the British Transport Police had 1,200 officers patrolling the subway system, Underground stations had 28 specially trained, explosive-sniffing dogs, and 700 officers from London's Metropolitan Police Service traveled on the bus network, terrorists mirrored the July 7 attacks with another strike. Minor explosions on July 21, that reportedly involved detonators only, forced three subway lines to close down, and there was another blast on a double-decker bus. Although there was only one minor injury and little damage caused, the implications were mind-numbing. Either extremists were trying to show their

ATTACKS ON THE RISE

According to RAND Corporation statistics, there were 5,362 deaths from terrorism worldwide between March 2004 and March 2005. This was almost double the total for the same 12-month period before the invasion of Iraq in 2003. (The RAND Corporation is a nonprofit research organization in the U.S.)

disregard for heightened security or London was falling prey to publicity-seeking terrorist mimics. On July 23, a bomb attack in the Egyptian Red Sea resort of Sharm el-Sheik claimed at least 64 lives. Was this a sign of renewed attacks to come?

By July 29, police had four bombing suspects in custody after armed raids in London and Rome. One of those arrested was Ibrahim Muktar Said, 27, wanted for an attempt to bomb a number 26 bus in Shoreditch, east London. Ramzi Mohamed, was suspected of an attempted bombing of the Oval Tube. Yassin Hassan Omar, 24, was suspected of the bomb attempt on the Tube near Warren Street. And the man arrested in Rome was Osman Hussain, 27, suspected in a bomb attempt at Shepherd's Bush station.

On August 4, Ayman al-Zawahri, reputedly the second in command of al-Qaeda, appeared in a pre-recorded video tape on Al-Jazeera television. Though al-Zawahri made no direct claim that al-Qaeda carried out the attack, he embraced the London suicide bombings and warned Britain that more destruction would likely be ahead.

"Blair has brought to you destruction in central London, and he will bring more of that, God willing," he said.

It was the seventh time since September 11, 2001, al-Zawahri used videotapes or audiotapes to speak for al-Qaeda. However, he wore a black turban for the first time in this tape, "a sign that it's time of war," according to Montasser el-Zayat, an Egyptian lawyer known to defend Islamic radicals, and who spent three years in prison with al-Zawahri.

Police raids were carried out in Medina and Riyadh only a few weeks after al-Zawahri's video broadcast. Evidently, Saudi Arabian authorities were still pressuring to capture al-Qaeda operatives there. On August 18, Saleh Mohammed al-Aoofi, allegedly Osama bin Laden's top leader in Saudi Arabia, was among six al-Qaeda militants killed in clashes. The raids also proved al-Qaeda was still very much alive in the Persian Gulf.

The coordinated nature of both sets of the London bombings held the chilling stamp of the terror group, just like the 2004 Madrid train bombings and the attack on the World Trade Center in 2001. The similarities were frighteningly obvious.

Terror in New York

While terrorism has been an historic fact in the Middle East for centuries, it only began to regularly make front-page headlines on western newspapers in May 1961. This date recorded the first hijacking of an American commercial aircraft, when a Puerto-Rican activist took over a jetliner and forced it to land in Cuba.

In January 1975, more Puerto-Rican separatists bombed Fraunces Tavern in lower Manhattan, killing four patrons and injuring 60 others. Two days later, homegrown terrorists, known as the Weather Underground, claimed responsibility for a bomb detonated in a bathroom in the State Department in New York.

Generally, Americans forgot about these attacks, and U.S. police forces discounted threats on their soil. This, despite the fact that in 1997 they had fielded rumors of terrorist plans to use planes as flying bombs, and in August 1998, the Federal Bureau of Investigation (FBI) received a report from the Central Intelligence Agency (CIA) alleging terrorists planned to use jet planes for an attack. Apparently, a Caribbean police official claimed that Libya hired an Islamic fundamentalist group to fly a plane packed with explosives into the World Trade Center. Indirectly, the United States received an advance warning for 9/11. Three years later, they experienced just such an attack.

The events began at 7:59 a.m. on September 11, 2001, when American Airlines Flight 11 lifted off from the tarmac in Boston, bound for Los Angeles. Fifteen minutes later, at 8:14 a.m., United Airlines Flight 175 departed for the same destination. At 8:20 a.m. American Airlines Flight 77 left Washington's Dulles Airport, bound for Los Angeles, and at 8:42 a.m. United Airlines Flight 93 took off from Newark destined for San Francisco. At the time, no one knew of the terror these flights would stir.

American Airlines Flight 11

During her 12-year career as a veteran airline attendant, Madeline Sweeney faced all sorts of emergencies, but the perilous situation on American Airlines Flight 11's Boeing 767, with its 92 passengers and crew on board that morning, was her final one.

At 8:14 a.m., air traffic controllers at Logan Airport ordered American Airlines Flight 11 to turn right. The pilot responded as usual. Strangely, however, the pilot ignored the controller's subsequent command for the plane to climb to 35,000 feet (10,700 m) in altitude a few minutes later. By then, American Airlines Flight 11 likely already was hijacked.

About five minutes after the hijacking, flight attendant Betty Ong contacted the American Airlines southeastern reservations office in Cary, North Carolina. Using an AT&T air phone, she reported the emergency aboard the flight. Ong spoke for about 25 minutes, calmly describing the events onboard the craft. Also, at 8:25 a.m. and again at 8:29 a.m., Sweeney contacted Michael Woodward, the Logan Airport ground manager. Sweeney managed to telephone Woodward after her first call was cut-off.

"This plane has been hijacked," she whispered into her mouthpiece, panic etching her words. She reported that two flight attendants had been stabbed (most likely by Wail al-Shehri and Waleed al-Shehri, who were seated in row two in first class), and it appeared they also killed a passenger. While Sweeney spoke, the plane veered south.

At 8:20 a.m., Boston flight control suspected Flight 11 had been hijacked. They followed its progress on their scope, but a minute later, the bright American Airlines Flight 11 blip disappeared from their screen. Someone onboard turned off the transponder. Protocol in such situations is for traffic control to notify North American Air Defense Command (NORAD) immediately, but for some reason, in the confusion and uncertainty of the moment, they did not notify NORAD of the strange flight pattern until 8:28 a.m.

At 8:46:40 a.m., American Airlines Flight 11 struck the 110-story North Tower of the World Trade Center just above the 90th floor. The impact of the collision killed everyone onboard instantly and ignited the 20,000 gallons (75,708 liters) of jet fuel in the airplane's tanks. The resulting fireball raised temperatures in the area impacted to a searing 2,000 degrees Fahrenheit (1,093° Celsius).

United Airlines Flight 175

At 8:14 a.m., United Airlines Flight 175, a Boeing 767 with nine crew and 56 passengers, departed Logan Airport. Nineteen minutes later, it gained cruising altitude of 31,000 feet (9,450 m). Between 8:42 a.m. and 8:46 a.m., terrorist actions on United Airlines Flight 175 mimicked those on American Airlines Flight 11. At 8:52 a.m., passenger Peter Hanson called his father to report the hijacking.

"I think they've taken over the cockpit—an attendant has been stabbed—and someone else up front may have been killed. The plane is making strange moves. Call United Airlines—tell them it's Flight 175, Boston to L.A."

At the same time, a male flight attendant also reported the hijacking to the United Airlines office in San Francisco. By 8:58 a.m., the aircraft deviated from its course and turned south.

At 9:00 a.m., Hanson made a second phone call. "It's getting bad, Dad—a stewardess was stabbed—they seem to have knives and mace—they said they have a bomb—it's getting very bad on the plane—passengers are throwing up and getting sick—the plane is making jerky movements—I don't think the pilot is flying the plane—I think we are going down—I think they intend to go to Chicago or someplace and fly into a building—don't worry, Dad—If it happens, it'll be very fast—my God, my God."

At 9:03:11 a.m., United Airlines Flight 175 crashed into the southeast corner of the World Trade Center's South Tower.

Two purposefully controlled crashes began a cascading series of structural failures in the twin towers and soon brought them crumbling to earth. The events shook the world, as well. Terrorists successfully struck a symbol of America's economic power, intent on murdering the 45,000 people working in the World Trade Center towers. The actions resulted in 2,752 deaths.

American Airlines Flight 77

At 8:20 a.m., American Airlines Flight 77, a Boeing 757 bound from Washington Dulles to Los Angeles, took off with six crew and 58 passengers. Sometime between 8:51 a.m. and

8:54 a.m., hijackers took control of the plane, which deviated from its course. Several passengers made phone calls to alert authorities.

At 9:29 a.m., the hijackers turned off the autopilot on American Airlines Flight 77. The aircraft, flying at 7,000 feet (2,100 m), was about 38 miles (61 km) west of Washington, D.C. Within five minutes, the plane was only five miles (eight km) west-southwest and descending 2,200 feet (670 m) toward downtown Washington. At 9:37:46 a.m., flying at full throttle, the aircraft dove into the Pentagon.

United Airlines Flight 93

At 8:42 a.m., United Airlines Flight 93 left Newark (New Jersey) Liberty International Airport, bound for San Francisco. The flight was 25 minutes late, with 37 passengers on board.

By all accounts, the crew spent the first 46 minutes of United Airlines Flight 93 carrying out their regular routine, but at 9:28 a.m., hijackers attacked. The plane suddenly lost 700 feet

(213 m) in altitude, dropping from 35,000 feet (10,700 m) over eastern Ohio amid radio transmissions from the pilot declaring a "Mayday," with the sounds of a struggle in the background.

Ten passengers made phone calls to their loved ones, describing the situation. The passengers onboard United Airlines Flight 93 heard news of the crashes in New York, and at some point, the passengers attempted to retake control of their plane. At 9:57 a.m., they launched a sustained assault.

Apparently trying to knock the passengers off balance, the hijacking pilot rolled the plane left and right. When that didn't work, he pitched the nose of the plane upward and downward. The passengers kept up their frantic charge of the cockpit door, until the pilot decided to crash. The hijackers shouted, "Allah is the greatest. Allah is the greatest." Then, the hijacking pilot rolled the airplane onto its back and dove into an empty field in Shanksville, Pennsylvania, at 580 miles (933 km) per hour.

Terror in Japan

On March 20, 1995, Aum Shinrikyo (Supreme Truth), a cult led by 40-year-old Shoko Asahara, attempted to spread the poison sarin—one of the world's most toxic chemicals—through Japan's heavily congested subway systems in Tokyo and Yokohama. This was not the first terrorist attempt on Japan. In the 1970s, the Japanese Red Army mounted terrorist attacks, but at the time, the threat was directed primarily at targets overseas. With Aum Shinrikyo, the threat was ominously intimate to Japan.

At 8:05 a.m., Aum Shinrikyo launched the subway attack. Disguised as commuting businessmen, cult members simultaneously put 10 sarin-filled plastic bags on trains headed for Tokyo's central station. As the trains approached the station, one member of each team allegedly punctured the bag with the sharpened tip of an umbrella, while another cult member kept a watch for observers. The sarin flowed from the bags, silently ready to poison train passengers. The clear liquid evaporated slowly, and all but one of the terrorists had enough time to escape.

As the poisonous fumes spread through the packed train cars and crowded rush-hour platforms, the effects overcame hundreds of innocent commuters. They staggered, vomited, and collapsed in 16 stations along the three subway lines targeted by the attack. By the time the gas dissipated, 12 people were dead and more than 5,700 injured.

Japan's sarin attack drew global attention because the country faced incredibly narrow deadlines for preemptive action. The Japanese government acted swiftly, performing a nationwide sweep that snagged the cult leadership, as well as tons of chemicals for sarin manufacture and $7 million cash intended to fund the Aum Shinrikyo's terrorist strategy.

The ominous attack in Japan reminded the intelligence community of the public's vulnerability to biological warfare. Apparently, terrorists could procure and employ worse toxins than sarin. For example, VX, a deadly nerve agent first developed by U.S. scientists in the 1950s, can persist on the ground for several weeks and pose a long-term contamination hazard. Much more dangerous than other more volatile chemical substances and 10 times more lethal than sarin, VX could kill if inhaled or touched to the skin.

The Biological Threat

In December 1991, the Union of Soviet Socialist Republics (USSR) separated into 15 individual countries. The global intelligence community knew the fall of the USSR readily made available the expertise terrorists needed for chemical or biological attacks. Scores of loose geeks and spooks (scientists and spies) formerly employed in the USSR were looking for work. Some had been employed by Biopreparat, the USSR's major bioweapons facility. With the dissolution of the USSR in 1991, Biopreparat suffered dramatic downsizing, and more than half of its scientific staff departed. Many left Russia for laboratories in the West.

Biopreparat was established in 1973, one year after the USSR signed the Biological and Toxin Weapons Convention. By the 1980s, the company produced the bulk of biotechnology in the USSR. Using a civilian pharmaceutical and vaccine company as a cover, the biological weapons work consisted of some 40 research-and-production facilities, including a dozen major complexes. Staff duties included new weapons development and finding cures and antidotes.

At its peak, estimates suggest that Biopreparat had at least 47 labs and test facilities scattered across Russia, and the company employed more than 40,000 workers, including 9,000 scientists, of which 1,000 to 2,000 were deadly pathogens experts. In 1989, U.S. intelligence agencies got their first look behind the curtain of secrecy surrounding Biopreparat. Biopreparat employee Vladimir Pasechnik revealed that the Soviet biological warfare effort was 10 times larger than previously estimated by U.S. or British intelligence.

In 1992, Dr. Kanatjan Alibekov (Ken Alibek) defected. He confirmed Pasechnik's reports by providing even more detail about Moscow's extensive biological warfare development program. According to Alibekov, Biopreparat manufactured 4,960 tons of anthrax, along with highly virulent forms of smallpox. Both could be used as biological weapons.

Bioweapons in the United States

In the United States, the FBI knew of shifting styles in terrorist attacks. The first evidence that biological warfare was a threat occurred in The Dalles, Oregon, in 1984. Followers of the Bhagwan Shree Rajneesh religious cult contaminated restaurant salad bars with a homegrown version of salmonella (*Salmonella Typhimurium*).

Some 750 people became ill, with 45 requiring hospitalization.

The 1993 World Trade Center underground parking lot bomb is another example of readily available biological poisons in use. Allegedly, the bomb was laced with cyanide. After the court case that sent the World Trade Center-parkade terrorists to jail, U.S. district court sentencing judge, Kevin Duffy, said, "Thank God the sodium cyanide burned instead of vaporizing [or] everybody in the North Tower would have been killed."

What made the situation even more dangerous, according to antiterrorism experts, was the fact that information about how to manufacture biological poisons was available through services such as the Internet. One resource, *Uncle Fester's Silent Death*, included recipes for shellfish toxin, botulism, and Ricin. The *Jolly Roger Cookbook* spread information about making fertilizer bombs and propellants. *Terrorist Handbook* and *Anarchy Cookbook* also provided similar how-to instruction. Such resources have proliferated.

In 1993, the Canadian Border Patrol stopped Thomas Lewis Lavy, an American with reported ties to survivalist groups. He attempted to smuggle 4.5 ounces (130 grams) of Ricin, another deadly chemical, from Alaska into Canada.

In a different incident, on February 28, 1995, a court convicted Douglas Baker and Leroy Wheeler of the right-wing Minnesota Patriots Council for the unlawful possession of biological weapons—specifically Ricin. In May of the same year, Larry Wayne Harris, who allegedly had ties to the white supremacist group Aryan Nation, was arrested for ordering three vials of freeze-dried bubonic plague bacteria from the American Type Culture Collection in Maryland.

Obviously, acts of terrorism using biological or chemical weapons posed a growing threat. In addition, a study released in July 2003 by the Partnership for Public Service in the United States, indicated that half of the

federal scientific and medical personnel working in jobs that supported the biodefense mission could retire over the next five years. There
was little extra effort being made to replace their
expertise with fresh blood. America was becom-
ing more vulnerable all the time. Experts spread
more gloom with questions about America's
food supply.

Protecting the U.S. Food Supply

 Food production accounts for nearly 10 percent of the U.S. gross domestic product. Pro-
ducing the food Americans eat generates nearly
$1 trillion in cash receipts and employs one in
eight American workers. Among the largest
agricultural sectors is the $90-billion livestock
industry. What would happen if anthrax or
another disease was introduced to this industry? Experts worried that if a contagious disease,
such as foot-and-mouth, broke out in cattle
herds around Amarillo, Texas, up to 1.5 million
head of cattle located within a 100-mile (161 km)

radius would have to be slaughtered. Terrorists didn't have to strike human targets to severely impact Americans and the U.S. economy.

Experts also warned that terrorists could use even deadlier materials in acts of bioterror, yet there was no federal program in place at the time to provide ongoing supervision of lethal pathogen handling. Many university research labs around the country held highly contagious specimens, but often there was a lax level of security at the universities. In 2002, for example, federal inspectors found seven vials of the pathogens that cause bubonic plague and pneumonic plague in an unlocked refrigerator at one university. A university lecturer supposedly had custody of the vials, but he had not inventoried the freezer since 1994.

These situations lent credibility to concerns by antiterrorism experts. Bioweapon particles are invisible to the unaided human eye. Each particle is only one to five microns in diameter—a micron being equal to one-fiftieth the width of a human hair. There is usually no odor or taste to alert a victim that an attack is underway. If terrorists managed an effective means of dispersing bioweapons, it would create enormous havoc. When pneumonic plague becomes airborne, it is nearly 100 percent fatal. Its victims usually die within 48 hours. According to a 2003 study of emergency response to a hypothetical anthrax attack, the release of just two pounds (1 kg) of weapons-grade anthrax dropped on an American city could result in more than 100,000 deaths.

Even so, authorities were reluctant to speak out about the threat of bioweapons. They apparently didn't feel terrorist groups had the technological capability to use these weapons and likely had no way to disperse chemicals or biological toxins effectively. For example, they needed nine tons of a "highly toxic" agent, such as Ricin, to cover a 39-square-mile (100 sq km) area and cause 50 percent lethality. Deploying such an agent over a wide area, although possible, was impractical from a logistics standpoint, authorities believed, even for a well-funded organization. So why create undue concern when there were even more alarming worst-case scenarios to consider?

Chemicals and Vulnerability

At one time, chemical facilities laced the United States, providing a potentially cost-effective means for terrorist attacks.

About 15,000 chemical plants, refineries, and other sites in the United States stored large quantities of hazardous materials on their property. In the period before September 11, only 21 percent of the sites employed basic security measures, such as posted warning signs, fencing, access control, and full-time surveillance. The U.S. Environmental Protection Agency (EPA) estimated there were 823 sites where the death or injury toll from a catastrophic disaster at a chemical plant could reach from 100,000 to more than 1 million people in a worst-case scenario.

Another report, issued by the Council on Foreign Relations, concluded that the United States was also dangerously unprepared to defend itself against other types of terrorism. As late as 1998, the FBI only had two members who could translate documents written in Arabic, for example. This huge hole in capability left the FBI with stacks of intercepted telephone conversations between Islamic terror suspects that were not translated for use by prosecutors and investigators.

Aware of potential terrorist danger, the U.S. government spent more money in an effort to prevent terrorist acts of a biological and chemical nature. The 2005 federal budget continued implementation of the Project BioShield initiative, which allowed the government to purchase critically needed vaccines and medications for biodefense. The Strategic National Stockpile contained drugs, vaccines, and other medical supplies and equipment for delivery anywhere in the country within 12 hours.

For 2005, the federal budget requested $2.5 billion for BioShield, compared with $0.9 billion in 2004. High on the list for purchases were next-generation vaccines for both smallpox and anthrax. Bioterrorism was a grave concern, but there was still potential for more terrorist-caused disasters of another nature.

The Nuclear Threat

What would happen if a single-engine Cessna crashed into a critical facility such as a nuclear power plant? Although such an event has not occurred in the United States, on August 14, 2003, an estimated 40 million Americans and 10 million Canadians learned firsthand what might happen should terrorists take aim at the power grid. At 4:10 p.m., the northeastern United States and parts of Canada suffered the largest blackout in U.S. history. The blackout began as a result of a series of faults along Lake Erie in Ohio. Three power lines sagged and came into contact with unpruned treetops in

Ohio, disrupting electrical power in eight states from Michigan to New York, as well as Ontario, Canada. The result was a domino effect of power failures in 263 power plants over just seven minutes.

The faults caused a cascading event that tripped off a large number of transmission lines, destabilizing part of the grid and creating a blackout. It took only 2½ hours to darken the lives of 50 million people and three days for the utilities to re-energize the transmission and distribution system.

Following September 11, 2001, U.S. authorities gave several indications of credible threats to the nation's nuclear power plants. Ten days after September 11, the Nuclear Regulatory Commission (NRC) issued a news release stating the commission had not considered this sort of threat to nuclear power plants. It said, "... the NRC did not specifically contemplate attacks by aircraft such as Boeing 757s or 767s and nuclear plants were not designed to withstand such crashes. Detailed engineering analyses of a large airline crash have not yet been performed."

On January 23, 2002, as an example, U.S. intelligence agencies issued internal alerts. Just six days later, in his State of the Union address, President George W. Bush revealed that diagrams of U.S. nuclear plants were found at al-Qaeda bases in Afghanistan.

Antiterrorism experts understood the potential of terrorists used low-grade radioactive material in a so-called "dirty bomb." They worried about what might happen if terrorists procured a supply of such material. This seemed a genuine threat after the collapse of the USSR. Although historic arms treaties enforced the decommissioning of nuclear missiles, the collapse may have left a huge storehouse of potentially lethal radioactive material accessible to terrorists.

While Russia and the former Soviet states reportedly had a firm grip on their nuclear stockpile, evidence suggested the safeguards were failing. While the Soviet's kept the development of suitcase nuclear bombs top secret, environmental advisor Alexei Yablokov, who was highly placed in the Boris Yeltsin administration, reportedly estimated that former USSR scientists created 132 such weapons. Russia, at the time of Yeltsin's administration, could only account for the whereabouts of 48. Special nuclear weapons, RA-115 and RA-115-01, better known as suitcase nuclear weapons, were a perfect example.

In 1996, the Massachusetts Institute of Technology Press (MIT Press) reported that since 1992, more fissile material was stolen from the former USSR than the United States produced in the first three years of the Manhattan Project. According to some authorities, separated plutonium and highly enriched uranium was so prevalent around the world at that time that it could be used to make thousands of nuclear weapons. In fact, weapons-grade nuclear materials existed in more than 130 research laboratories operating in over 40 countries; monitoring which acquired separated plutonium and highly enriched uranium for terrorism purposes became a priority to the intelligence community.

Radioactive material that could be employed in a dirty bomb was also available in industrial and medical equipment. For example, americium-241 is a radioactive material contained in devices used in the Azerbaijani oil fields. The radioactivity of cesium-137 devices, such as those found in high-dose brachytherapy units or portable X-ray weld-inspection devices, was common throughout the world, as well. Though such devices had a relatively low radioactivity wallop that would not produce sudden death, materials such as cesium-137 were nonetheless dangerous.

Not only foreign extremists but also homegrown terrorists in the United States and Canada could find radioactive material easily. The United States and Canada reportedly had more than 2 million licensed sources of radiological

materials—with over half a million near or beyond the end of their service life. According to
one authority, 300 sources of radiation were reported lost or stolen on an annual basis since
1996, and 56 percent were never recovered. In
fact, by the end of 2001, there were 5,000 "or-
phaned" radiation sources in the United States
alone. By then, the FBI carefully monitored its
own domestic crop of potential terrorists.

Homegrown Terror

On December 2, 1956, a bomb ripped through
a crowded movie theatre in Brooklyn, New
York. Such murders occurred infrequently, but
Americans knew the sorrow of bomb attacks
nonetheless.

In the late-1970s, Theodore John Kaczynski, known by the FBI as the Unabomber, began
attacking universities and airlines with explosives. In 1998, Kaczynski received a life sentence
without possibility of parole or appeal.

On July 27, 1996, Eric Robert Rudolph detonated a blast at Olympic Park during the Atlanta Olympics, killing one person and injuring more than 100 others. He also set off a remote-controlled bomb at a Birmingham, Alabama, abortion clinic that killed an off-duty police officer and maimed a nurse. On July 17, 2005, Rudolph received two life sentences without parole for the abortion-clinic bombing. In August 2005, he received four life terms in prison for the deadly Olympic bombing. Rudolph faced a possible death sentence, but received a plea deal in exchange for revealing the location of more than 220 pounds (100 kg) of stolen dynamite he had buried in North Carolina.

In the mid-1990s, Americans experienced the type of politically motivated terrorist attack that Islamic extremists employed in other parts of the world. Radicals believed that the United Nations and a covert international Jewish conspiracy called the Zionist Occupied Government (ZOG) spawned a New World Order that helped to create a domestic-terrorism threat in the United States. There was a mélange of para-military "militia" organizations, many of them anchored by a survivalist mission to be armed and self-sustaining in the event of U.S. government collapse, in nearly every state. For example, in the mid-western United States, desperate financial circumstances for farmers spawned activists to take terrorist action.

Two men, Timothy James McVeigh and his accomplice, Terry Nichols, blamed the economic situation on the U.S. government. On April 19, 1995, McVeigh killed 168 people with a truck bomb in Oklahoma City, Oklahoma.

None of the passersby on that morning had any cause to wonder about a large yellow Ryder Truck Rental truck parked in front of the Alfred P. Murrah Federal Building. But at 9:02 a.m., the truck disintegrated, ripping away the core of the 7-story building and shattering windows 10 blocks away. A 4,000-pound (1,800 kg) homemade bomb—a mix of fertilizer and fuel oil—filled the truck.

In the weeks leading up to the Oklahoma bombing, U.S. law enforcement and intelligence officials received several warnings from informants that Islamic terrorists planned to strike somewhere in the United States. The United States Marshals Service concluded the attack might involve suicide bombers. Separately, the General Service Administration also received threats that federal buildings were to be the targets of terrorist attacks. So when the Murrah building bombing occurred, antiterrorism officials logically concluded that Islamic extremists conducted the attack.

Within a few hours of the blast, eight terrorist groups claimed responsibility for the Oklahoma-City bombing. Fearing more attacks, many cities across the country closed their federal buildings, including Boston, Boise, Cincinnati, Steubenville, Fort Worth, Omaha, Portland, Rochester, and Wilmington.

While the CIA, National Security Agency, Counterterrorism Center, and the National

Reconnaissance Office scoured data for information about radical Islamic suspects—apparently identifying more than 100 foreigners as possible perpetrators—a state trooper named Charles J. Hanger stopped a motorist for a traffic violation 75 miles (121 km) north of Oklahoma City on I-35. The state trooper pulled over McVeigh's 1977 Mercury Grand Marquis because it did not have a license plate. Acting on his suspicions, the police officer noticed McVeigh was carrying a 9-mm Glock without a valid permit. He detained McVeigh on four misdemeanor charges.

Information about McVeigh's arrest went unnoticed as the FBI followed the belief that the Islamic Jihad was the group responsible for the attack. They launched an international dragnet for young men traveling alone to the Middle East, which resulted in the arrest of Abraham Abdallah Ahmed, a Jordanian-American living in Oklahoma City. Ahmed happened to be traveling to Jordan, dressed in a track suit similar to one reportedly worn by a man near the scene of the bombing. They took other men of Middle-Eastern origin into custody, as well. One, a cab-driver from Queens, was traveling with two others who had stopped to ask directions from an Oklahoma highway patrolman.

Two days passed before the FBI traced the fragments of a vehicle identification number taken from the axle of the truck they believed was involved in the explosion. They managed to trace the truck to a Ryder dealership in Junction City, Kansas, where McVeigh had rented it under an alias—Robert Kling. With eye witnesses helping, the FBI compiled a composite drawing of the suspect. After canvassing motels in the area, the police identified Timothy McVeigh as the truck driver. A records' search showed he was in the custody of the Noble County Jail in Perry, Oklahoma.

One of the most expensive trials in the country's history opened to media fanfare on April 24, 1997. McVeigh and Nichols received separate trials, and after a lengthy court session, a jury took three days of deliberation to determine that McVeigh caused the Murrah-building explosion. McVeigh received a death sentence for each of the 11 counts in his indictment. His sentence was carried out on June 11, 2001.

CHAPTER 3

The Al-Qaeda Network

Most acts of terror against the West were limited to the third world, until Islamic fundamentalist Ruhollah Mousavi, the Ayatollah Khomeini, rose to power in Iran. Khomeini became the Henry Ford of Islamic terrorism, thanks to mosques around the world.

The majority of Muslims are *Sunni*, the minority *Shia*. The minority regards Ali ibn Abi Talib, the prophet Muhammad's cousin and son-in-law, and his descendents as divinely authorized to rule the Muslim community. The majority group believes that the community should appoint the ruler, or caliph, through the consensus.

A Shi'ite Muslim, Khomeini believed in an extreme form of the Shia creed. Shi'ites practiced something akin to the separation of church and state for centuries. Khomeini called for a clerical state to succeed the "corrupt" Shah throughout the 1960s and 1970s. From exile, he built a strong power base among his religious followers within the country. In 1978, a series of student demonstrations rocked the Shah's regime, weakening his control. The following year, the Shah fled to U.S. protection and Khomeini seized power.

Khomeini appointed himself "supreme ruler," with a "parliament" made up of clerics directed from Tehran. Khomeini instituted a strict regime of Islamic law. He ordered women to wear veils and suspended the criminal justice system in favor of religious courts. He put a democratic apparatus in place for appearances only.

Once securely in power, Khomeini created one of the time's most dangerous international terrorist groups. The group was called the *Hezbollah* (Party of God). Khomeini mass produced recruiting materials and used mosques to spread the word to the faithful.

Developing a U.S. Authority on Terrorism

In response, as early as 1983, U.S. President Ronald Regan designated the FBI as the lead domestic counterterrorism agency in the United States. Though the FBI was charged with the duty, it appeared the apprehension of domestic criminals was still their primary focus. The proof was the fact that students at the FBI Academy received only three days of counterterrorism training in their four-month course at Quantico, Virginia.

Without a more obvious effort by the FBI to

stop the recruitment of insurgents, Khomeini's actions spawned groups dedicated to the downfall of western Christian governments. In the mid-1980s, a group founded by Abu Nidal (Sa bri al-Banna) after a split with the Palestinian Liberation Organization, slipped beneath the radar of western intelligence agencies. There was an Abu Nidal "sleeper" network of terrorists implanted deep within U.S. society, waiting for a command to act. In 1986, the Abu Nidal network, along with another cell of the same group, was discovered by the CIA. In the fall of that year, the CIA monitored a meeting of Abu Nidal operatives in the Mediterranean area. They identified one attendee, a nondescript Palestinian Arab named Zein al-Abdeen Hassan Isa, who was living in St. Louis, Missouri. After the meeting, the CIA followed Isa, and closely observed his activities. Using telephone wiretaps and surveillance, CIA agents uncovered another substantial Abu Nidal operative network.

By the mid-1990s, footwork by the FBI

uncovered yet another network of "sleepers." This one, however, was not run by the Abu Nidal. It was a faction of the Hezbollah. While dangerous, the Hezbollah would not become known to the world as the worst terrorist menace in history. This infamous accolade would be held by a group called al-Qaeda, formed by an extremist Muslim named Osama bin Laden.

The Birth of Al-Qaeda

To understand the foundations of al-Qaeda, one must examine the life of its founder. Usama bin Mohammed bin Laden, commonly known as Osama bin Laden, was born in 1957 in Riyadh, Saudi Arabia, but his ancestral home was in the desolate Hadramout region of south-central Yemen. His father, Mohammed, was born to poverty in the village of al-Ribat.

In the late 1920s, Mohammed bin Awad bin Laden and two of his brothers walked out of Husn Bahishn, their hometown at the head of the remote Yemeni valley of the Wadi Du'an.

In search of a better life, the brothers joined a camel caravan bound for Jeddah, the gateway to Mecca on the Red Sea. The arduous 1,000-mile (1,600 km) journey was not easy. In fact, it claimed the life of one brother.

Blind in his right eye, Mohammed was a tall, dark man with a pockmarked face. He could neither read nor write; indeed, he couldn't even sign his name. He worked as a porter on the docks in Jeddah, a transit port for pilgrims on their way to perform *hajj*, the pilgrimage to the nearby holy city of Mecca. After two years on the docks, Mohammed had a chance encounter with an investor who wished to purchase land in Jeddah.

Mohammed arranged the land sale and earned a sizeable commission. He sought to use his profit by investing in Jeddah's booming economy. Jeddah needed skilled construction workers. In 1931, he became a Jeddah bricklayer with a modest construction company. Quickly, Mohammed learned all he needed to know to grow his own business. Within two years, the one-time dock porter was employing hundreds of laborers, and he was a businessman of substance in Jeddah. While Mohammed's construction enterprise continued to grow in the following years, one daring project transformed Bin Laden Construction into a megalithic building concern.

The Growth of Bin Laden Construction

The al-Saud family wrestled political control of Saudi Arabia, and in 1948, King Abd al-Aziz bin Abd al-Rahman bin Faysal al-Saud was in the market for a palace. King Abd al-Aziz thought a central administration for the government unnecessary. In fact, from the 1920s to 1940s in the capital city, Riyadh, the government consisted of fewer than a dozen foreign advisors. To show his rule was not autocratic or out of touch with his people, however, the king regularly reverted to an informal kind of Bedouin democracy. With *majilis*, informal councils open to any of his subjects, King Abd al-Aziz tried to keep abreast of what his subjects were thinking. Mohammed took every opportunity to attend these councils, and he sat as near as possible to the king.

By that time, Mohammed already worked on several palaces for members of the royal family. At the majilis, he convinced the aging, arthritic king of his skill as a builder. Climbing stairs was difficult for the king, so Mohammed suggested that King Abd al-Aziz build a new palace with a car ramp that led up the outside wall to the first-floor bedrooms. Mohammed coaxed the king with stories about a palace that people could look to proudly as a physical testament to the al-Saud family's courage and power.

Prior to gaining oil riches, funds in the royal treasury were meager. The cost of an architectural tribute, such as the palace Mohammed had in mind, would quickly drain the funds. Acting on a hunch that the al-Saud's control of his adopted country would result in further economic expansion and opportunities,

Mohammed decided to pursue the palace contract. He supplied plans for a lavish $6-million structure that rose from behind high walls on the outskirts of Riyadh—a palace envied the world over. King Abd al-Aziz immediately wanted to build the palace. Estimates suggest that Bin Laden Construction lost at least $3 million during the protracted building process of the palace.

As a result of his $3-million sacrifice, Mohammed earned the close friendship of the al-Saud family. Soon, he received a contract to build one of the first major roads in the kingdom—from Jeddah to Medina.

In November 1953, King Abd-al-Aziz died and was succeeded by Crown Prince Saud Bin-Abd-al-Aziz Al Saud. The new king's brother, Faysal was named crown prince.

King Saud Abd al-Aziz Al Saud, a spendthrift, continued the tradition of his father's lavishness, using Bin Laden Construction to build so many projects that the company became one of the most powerful in the country.

The king's habit of showy spending—he was known to drive through the streets of Riyadh in his Rolls-Royce Cornish tossing gold coins to his subjects—eventually took its toll on the royal treasury. Although oil that had been discovered in 1938 provided a positive cash flow to the country, the price of oil was minute compared to later years. At the time, crude oil sold for about $19 per barrel compared to about $66 today. By March 22, 1958, the situation nearly became intolerable. When Prince Faysal took over the reins of government as the prime minister, he found the paltry sum of only 317 riyals—less than $100—in the state treasury.

No longer a privileged benefactor, Prince Faysal made private appeals for loans just to maintain his household. Mohammed lent Prince Faysal money to support the extended royal family, while Prince Faysal fought to gain control of Saudi-Arabian finances from the king. In 1963, King Abd al-Aziz and Prince Faysal struggled for power, and by 1964, Faysal deposed Saud after Mohammed helped convince King Abd al-Aziz to step down from the throne. In 1960, Saudi Arabia became a founding member of the Organization of Petroleum Exporting Countries (OPEC), so Mohammed knew his future was golden under King Faysal. In gratitude for his generosity, the king appointed Mohammed minister of public works, thereby making Mohammed's company the preferred contractor for a large number of capital projects in the country. Mohammed built holy mosques in Mecca and Medina, and handled construction projects from highways and bridges to airports.

A Growing Family

While Mohammed grew his company, his family also ballooned in numbers. Living according to the traditions of his desert forebears, Mohammad kept four wives, one of which he married and divorced with some regularity, a commonplace act in Saudi upper society.

Reportedly, Mohammed sired 24 sons and 30 daughters. Osama's mother, Alia Ghanem, was one of Mohammed's four wives. Mohammed discovered the daughter of a hard-working Syrian family during a business trip to Damascus. He quickly arranged the marriage to the 22-year-old woman. Alia bore Osama, Mohammed's 17th child.

When Osama was six months old, the family moved to Medina. Mohammed argued loudly and often with his new wife. Married relatively late in life by Middle-Eastern standards, Alia had a mind of her own. She did not listen well to her traditional Arab husband. She often refused to accept life in his strictly religious household. By the time the family moved, Mohammed barely tolerated Alia. She suffered isolation and was ostracized by the rest of the family. Mohammed's many children and his other wives viciously ridiculed the woman, calling her *Al Abeda*—the slave. As Osama grew older, he took the derisive nickname of *Ibn Al Abeda*—son of a slave.

Mohammed banished Alia to another household, but he allowed Osama to remain in Medina. Nannies and nurses raised Osama. His step-mother, Mohammed's first wife, Al-Khalifa, provided maternal influence, and he rarely saw his biological mother.

As he grew up, Osama tried to gain his father's attention. From an early age, Osama worked on roads built by Bin Laden Construction. However, gaining his father's respect and attention wasn't an easy task in the large household. Still, Mohammed showed genuine affection for his children equally, and once or twice a year he gave them all a chance to build a bond with him during a camping vacation in the desert. During those family retreats, Osama excelled. He loved the outdoors, and he enjoyed riding horses, shooting, and playing in the dunes. He was an adept hunter, much to his father's pride. However, Mohammed conducted business even during family vacations in the mountains. He often hosted clients of Bin

Laden Construction while on holiday. On several occasions, Osama foraged in the dunes of sand with the crown prince, Prince Abd al-Rahman. At the age of nine, the two young men became inseparable, as Osama instructed his playmate in the techniques of hunting and riding.

In 1967, when Osama was 10 years old, Mohammed was killed in an airplane crash, while inspecting a massive road construction project on the Saudi-Yemeni border. Quickly, rumors spread that the death had not been accidental (the investigation remains a Saudi government secret). After the accident, Osama repeatedly attempted to visit his young royal friend, but he never again had an audience with al-Rahman.

However, Mohammed's friendship with the al-Sauds was less feeble. When Mohammed died, King Faysal made a proclamation, announcing he considered Mohammed's offspring his children, thereby, more or less, adopting them all. Faysal appointed a *hadhrami*, Mohammed

Ba Harith, to run the bin Laden empire until the boys grew old enough to maintain the company. Eventually, Salem, Mohammed's eldest son, took control.

Salem attended Millfield, a private school in southern England, and he married Caroline Carey, an upper-class Englishwoman whose stepfather was the Marquis of Queensbury. A talented pilot and musician, Salem became a favorite of yet another ruler, King Fahd. King Fahd entrusted the bin Ladens with royal construction projects, as well. By the time Osama was a teenager, the Binladen Group, as it was later named, was well on its way to employing more than 37,000 people and pulling in annual earnings estimated at $5 billion.

Osama bin Laden's Foundations for Terror

As a child, Osama excelled in Koran studies. He found studying the Koran was the one way he could gain one-on-one time with Mohammed in Medina. It was natural for him to follow the strictures of his faith.

At 17 years of age, Osama married his first wife, his 14-year-old Syrian first cousin. Najwa was the first of Osama's four wives, and she bore him 11 children.

At 19, Osama enrolled in King Abdul-Aziz University in Jeddah, where he studied economics and business management. Osama was attracted to the growing pro-Islamic, anti-Western rhetoric building among Muslims in Arabia. Since he was a boy, Osama claimed to harbor feelings of hatred toward America.

Osama's mentors in the late 1970s advocated within the radical Muslim Brotherhood, including Palestinian-born Dr. Sheikh Abdullah Azzam, who taught jurisprudence. Azzam, a man whom *Time* magazine once called "the reviver of jihad [holy war] in the 20th century," spiced his lectures with calls for jihad. "Jihad and the rifle alone. No negotiation. No meetings. No dialogue. Jihad and the rifle alone…"

Azzam's rhetoric meshed well with Osama's opinions. In December 1979, the Soviet army invasion of Muslim Afghanistan fired Osama's religious indignation. The Soviets eventually killed more than a million Afghanistanis, forcing about 5 million into exile. The invasion marked the first time since World War II that a non-Muslim army occupied a Muslim country. Azzam passionately urged Islamic volunteers worldwide to go to Afghanistan and help defeat the invaders.

Osama left the university and was among the first to respond. Within days of the Soviet invasion, he traveled to Afghanistan to take part in the fight. Osama brought hundreds of tons of construction machinery to Afghanistan, which he put at the disposal of the mujahideen to build roads and dig tunnels into the mountains for shelter.

Not long after he arrived, Osama met with his mentor, Azzam. In the town of Banu in northern Pakistan, the two men pondered the job ahead of them. Muslims from every corner of the Middle East arrived to lend a hand to the mujahideen, but there was a state of organized chaos. They did not know where to go to join the fight nor did they have a place to stay.

At Azzam's urgings, Osama helped create a guesthouse in Peshawar for Muslims drawn to the jihad. He called it *Beit al-Ansar*, or House of the Supporters. About that time, Azzam also formed the *Maktab al-Khidamat lil Mujahidin* (the Afghan Services Bureau that became known as the MAK). The MAK was the support organization for Arab volunteers in Afghanistan. It eventually became the foundation of al-Qaeda.

Azzam seemed to fulfill a missing guidance role for Osama. He was outspoken, much like the father Osama had barely known. Azzam counseled Osama, sharing his vision of a new world-sweeping movement for Islam.

To feed the fight against the Soviets, the MAK advertised for recruits. Through 1986, Osama oversaw fundraising efforts that, over time, channeled several billion dollars from private contributions, governments, and charities to the MAK. Osama, a millionaire through his inheritance, provided financial assistance to the MAK, which opened recruiting offices in 50 countries. Thanks to Osama, the MAK also established a recruitment hub in Brooklyn at the Alkifah Refugee Center.

CIA observers knew of Osama, but considered the wealthy man no more than a "Gucci terrorist." He was, in their opinion, little more than a charity organizer and philanthropist. Reports the CIA received from men who worked with Osama indicated that few regarded him as having the skills to lead anything more than a fundraising effort. During this time, however, Osama forged tight links with high-ranking officials in both the Pakistani and Saudi government. The al-Saud family, however, knew of Osama's talents.

In the early 1980s, the Saudi royal family appealed to Osama to help create mujahideen

units to fight with Yemeni insurgents. Bank-
rolled by the Saudis, Osama personally oversaw the creation of an Arab volunteer group in
South Yemen. King Fahd was so delighted with
Osama's efforts that he reportedly agreed to
redouble Saudi Arabia's regular contributions
to fund the so-called "Afghan Arabs." In the
following 10 years, it was estimated that nearly
$2 billion in secret Saudi support funded the
mujahideen in Afghanistan.

Allegedly, Prince Turki bin Faysal bin Abdul-Aziz worked directly with Osama to channel
funds. To the al-Sauds, having radical Muslim
youth directing their activism abroad was much
better than dealing with the idle and jobless youth
who might foment trouble in their kingdom. At
the time, to encourage youth participation, Saudi
Arabia's national airline gave a 75 percent dis-
count as encouragement to any young men traveling to Afghanistan to fight in the holy war.

Around 1986, recruits arrived almost daily
in Pakistan. Osama's administration tracked

each one. They fed and housed recruits and helped them join the fray across the border. For Osama, being an administrator was not enough. His involvement in Afghanistan's war was so deeply entrenched that he acted on his own to take the MAK from a hostel type of organization to something much more ominous. With Azzam's approval, in 1986, Osama elevated the level of his military involvement.

Pakistan's Zia-ul-Haq government saw the Soviets in Afghanistan as a threat to their national security, but they shied from too public a show of support for the mujahideen, evidently fearing reprisals from Moscow. Osama decided to take advantage and help Pakistan affect military action as an intermediary. From 1980 to 1987, the head of Pakistan's 10,000-strong intelligence service—the Inter-Services Intelligence (ISI)—assisted the Afghan mujahideen with arms and training. Reportedly, General Akhtar Abdul Rahman regularly met with Osama in Peshawar to provide cash and intelligence.

Through the MAK, Osama helped train the flood of recruits for battle in Afghanistan. He built his first rudimentary military camp, named *al-Ansar*, at Jaji in Paktia province, a few miles from the place where Pakistan's north-west frontier juts into Afghanistan. Osama moved into a two-story villa in the suburb of University Town in Peshawar. He directed his operations like a field commander. Oth-

PROFILE OF AFGHANISTAN

Population: 26 million
Area: 251,773 sq miles
(652,225 sq km)
Capital: Kabul
Major languages: Pashto,
Dari (Persian)
Major religion: Islam
Life expectancy: 46 years

er secret camps for military training followed, including one called *al-Masadah*—the Lions' Den. By 1988, Osama established five more camps, all of which produced trained fighters for the mujahideen.

Osama himself, a tall man who stood head and shoulders over most of the recruits, took part in some of their battles, which reportedly included the battle of Jalalabad. The number

of recruits passing through his network of safe
houses was enormous, and Osama realized he
needed to track the "guesthouse" visitors and
recruits training in the camps. Estimates suggest that by 1994, between 15,000 and 20,000
young men left their countries to participate
in al-Qaeda training at camps in Afghanistan,
Sudan, Iran, and Yemen.

Forming the Base

Osama formed a network, which he named
al-Qaeda, or "the base." He set up al-Qaeda like
a corporation. Al-Qaeda had a command and
control structure in which members pledged
an oath of allegiance called *bayat*. Bayat was a
quasi-mediaeval oath of allegiance to the *emir*,
or leader. Regular internal investigations of
members and associates were to be conducted to detect informants, and when suspects
of collaboration were uncovered, they were to
be murdered.

While al-Qaeda associates may not have

pledged bayat to the group, they were none-theless important to its survival. The associates provided intelligence, money, equipment, and recruitment for the organization. An associate could be a part of a separate cell or organization, yet he might receive support, funding, and training through the al-Qaeda network.

In structure, al-Qaeda included a *majilis al shura* (consultation council), which considered, discussed, and approved major policies. A military committee, subordinate to the majilis al shura, approved military matters. A business committee handled the gathering of donations and the disbursement of funds to terrorist cells. Al-Qaeda also organized a *fatwah* (religious ruling) committee, which issued rulings on Islamic law.

By the second year of Osama's efforts, estimates suggest that 10,000 fighters received training in the MAK camps. Intelligence sources estimated that nearly half of the recruits came from Saudi Arabia; 3,000 from Algeria; 2,000 from Egypt, and the remaining from a mix of countries including Yemen, Pakistan, Sudan, Lebanon, Kuwait, Turkey, the United Arab Emirates (UAE), and Tunisia.

At the height of the Cold War with the USSR, the CIA saw this rampant recruitment as a handy way of meddling with the Soviet campaign in Afghanistan. The CIA launched a $500 million per year support effort in the form of arms and military expertise to train the impoverished and outgunned guerillas in their battle against the Soviets. Osama benefited from the American largesse. While recruits trained, Osama concentrated on fundraising in the Middle East. He successfully siphoned cash from his countrymen. In fact, at one point during the early years of the Afghanistan conflict, the MAK reportedly gathered up to $25 million each month in donations, thanks to Osama.

Heroes of the Jihad

In 1985, an Egyptian doctor traveled to Pakistan

to attend to Afghan refugees. The doctor, 34-year-old Ayman al-Zawahri, was the leader of Egypt's radical Islamic Jihad. When al-Zawahri treated Osama for high blood pressure, the two quickly bonded. Al-Zawahri was uncompromising in his radical interpretation of Islam, and he reinforced Osama's militant extremism. In Afghanistan, al-Zawahri found a soul mate in Osama.

Born on June 19, 1951, al-Zawahri was the son of a prominent doctor. He came from an upper-class neighborhood in Cairo, Egypt. An Islamic fundamentalist, al-Zawahri joined the outlawed Egyptian Islamic Jihad in the 1960s as a 16-year-old medical student. On one occasion, authorities arrested and charged him with being part of a Muslim Brotherhood plot to overthrow Egyptian president Gamal Abdel Nasser. After Anwar Sadat's election as Egyptian president, al-Zawahri worked to overthrow the leader. When Sadat made peace with Israel, members of the Egyptian Islamic Jihad assassinated the president, and al-Zawahri was arrested with other Islamic militants in a security sweep.

As defendant No. 113 in a 1981 trial, al-Zawahri was convicted on weapons charges but not for participating in the assassination plot. He received three years in prison. During his time in prison, al-Zawahri became a spokesperson for the Egyptian Islamic Jihad.

When the USSR left Afghanistan in 1989, a civil war between the Taliban and ambitious warlords gripped the

THE TALIBAN

The term literally means " students of Islam." This political group swept to power in Afghanistan in the mid-1990s. In 1996, when they captured the capital, Kabul, the outside world realized the Taliban's extreme Islamic policies, especially towards the place of women in society. After the Taliban's refusal to hand over Osama bin Laden, the U.S. initiated aerial attacks, paving the way for opposition groups to drive them from power in 2003. However, since the end of the war in Iraq, the Taliban have re-emerged as a fighting force, worsening the security situation in the east and south-east of Afghanistan.

country. Osama and Azzam had conflicting ideas about what action to take, resulting in arguments over Afghanistan's future. Azzam still encouraged jihad, but he wanted to build alliances with moderate Islamics, too, possibly causing the Afghan Arabs to enter a fight with Israel. Osama, however, wanted to focus the veterans on secular Muslim regimes before branching out to non-Muslim countries in the fight for Islam. Al-Zawahri shared Osama's vision and joined his efforts to direct al-Qaeda. Before long, Osama assumed total control over al-Qaeda.

On November 24, 1989, 45 pounds (20 kg) of TNT exploded in a car bomb at the entrance the Sabva-e-Leil Mosque in Peshawar, killing Azzam and his two sons during Friday prayers. Later, a Palestinian al-Qaeda member, Mohammad Saddiq Odeh, told American interrogators that Osama "personally ordered the killing of Azzam because he suspected his former mentor had ties with the Central Intelligence

Agency." Al-Zawahri, who delivered the eulogy
at Azzam's funeral, also said he thought Azzam
was an American agent.

Osama maintained his headquarters in Peshawar following the Soviet withdrawal, and his
support of Islamic extremists around the world
began to blossom. In November 1989, Islamic
fundamentalists took their fight to the streets
of New York.

Over four successive weekends in July
1989, the Special Operations Group of the FBI
observed men leaving the Alkifah Center at the
Al Farooq mosque in Brooklyn. The men traveled to a rifle range in Calverton, Long Island.
There, they practiced firing AK-47s and other
semi-automatic weapons, while the FBI captured the events on film. El Sayyid Nosair, a
34-year-old Egyptian immigrant, was among
the target shooters. Four months later, on November 5, Nosair allegedly shot Rabbi Mei-
er Kahane at Manhattan's Marriott Eastside
Hotel. Kahane was the founder of the radical

Kahane Chai and a former legislator in the Israeli parliament. The shooting happened in a room filled with witnesses.

Following the shooting, Nosair planned to run to a waiting taxi idling at the curb in front of the hotel. Target shooter Mahmud Abouhalima was to drive the taxi, but while Nosair was inside, hotel security ordered Abouhalima to move from the taxi stand. A Hispanic driver, Frank Garcia, from the Bronx, replaced Abouhalima's car.

Kahane's followers pursued Nosair after the shooting but couldn't catch him. Instead of a familiar face, he found an oblivious Garcia waiting in the taxi. Garcia casually drove away from the hotel for one block and then lawfully stopped for a red light. For obvious reasons, Nosair panicked. Leaping from the taxi in frustration, he sprinted toward Grand Central Station. Witnesses to Kahane's murder trailed behind him. Postal inspector Carlos Acosta happened to be standing near the station's entrance. Upon see-

ing the armed man waving his handgun, Acosta
drew his own gun. Nosair fired first, hitting the
postal inspector's bulletproof vest, but Acosta
maintained aim and fired back, injuring Nosair
in the neck. Police immediately arrested Nosair
and quickly swooped down on his rented house
in Cliffside Park, New Jersey.

At the house, the police found Mahmud
Abouhalima and a Palestinian named Mohammed Salameh. Scouring the house for more
detail on Nosair, the police gathered 47 boxes
of evidence, including 16 boxes of papers written mostly in Arabic. However, the police did
not link the murder and evidence to an act of
terrorism. Three days after the shooting, FBI
agents removed the boxes from New York police custody. Two days later, Manhattan district attorney Robert Morgenthau asserted his
jurisdiction over the murder case and had the
boxes moved to his office. They remained in the
district attorney's basement until Nosair's trial.
The prosecution's case against Nosair revolved

around eyewitness testimony, and the boxes never resurfaced during the trial. Investigators assumed the papers were of a religious nature. They learned otherwise a few years later. Police reviewed the contents of the boxes in 1993 and found they contained instructions on how to conduct assassinations, attack aircraft, and develop formulas for bomb making.

Despite eyewitness accounts of the shooting, the jury acquitted Nosair of Kahane's murder and the attempted murder of Acosta. Instead, they believed the defense's theory that Kahane's followers framed the accused. They found Nosair guilty of a minor gun possession charge and assault charges, and he was sent to prison. Judge Alvin Schlesinger gave Nosair the maximum sentence for each conviction and ordered the sentences served consecutively, adding up to 7½ years in prison. In a television documentary four years after the trial, Schlesinger described the jury's verdict as, "Totally against the weight of the evidence; it was irrational ... it just made no sense, common or otherwise, to have reached that verdict."

Back in Afghanistan, Osama entertained al-Qaeda supporters, including Prince Turki, Osama's financial connection to the Sauds. Prince Turki hoped to convince Osama to return to Saudi Arabia. Al-Zawahri could not return to Egypt for fear of imprisonment, so likely he remained in Pakistan.

At 32 years of age, Osama returned to the family business as a manager with Bin Laden Construction. He was a local folk hero in Riyadh because of his Afghanistan record. Saudi Prince Abdullah, the next in line for the Saudi crown, personally greeted Osama upon his return. Osama reveled in the notoriety, giving speeches about the great Afghan victory, to reinforce the myth of his leadership.

When Saddam Hussein invaded Kuwait in August 1990, Osama offered to help the al-Sauds organize an army of former Afghan Arab fighters to repel the Iraqis, should they have designs on the kingdom. He met with religious leaders to gain their support and began rounding up recruits who had returned to Saudi Arabia from the army of mujahideen. Osama's popularity appeared to be a matter of concern to the Saudi regime. Instead of accepting Osama's efforts, the Saudi government tried to curtail them and, instead, turned to the United States for help, allowing more than a half-million American troops onto Saudi soil.

The al-Saud royal family's power was based on the strict *Wahhabi* interpretation of Islam, which forbids non-Muslims from entering the holy mosques of Mecca and Medina. According to the tenets of the Wahhabi belief, nonbelievers are not encouraged to live in the country, and the family's decision to welcome American military offended Osama and other devout Muslims. Osama began lecturing against their decision and accused the royal family of desecrating Islam's birthplace. The Saudi internal secret service monitored his activity, which apparently prompted the royals to broker a secret deal with Osama.

According to the deal, the al-Sauds offered Osama a one-way visa out of the country with his four wives and growing family (by 2003 he had 15 children). Saudi Arabia might freeze his assets after his departure, and he could be publicly disavowed. However, in secret the al-Sauds may have agreed to continue to support Osama's personal jihad, providing he did not turn his mujahideen against them. Regardless of the deal's veracity, in 1991, Osama left Saudi Arabia and returned to Pakistan's al-Qaeda stronghold at Peshawar.

Once back on familiar ground, Osama unsuccessfully attempted to intervene in battles that erupted between opposing mujahideen factions in Afghanistan. Several times, Osama barely escaped attempts on his life. When he learned that the ISI, formerly his secret supporter, mounted a campaign to capture him, Osama probably realized that his revolution needed a safer place from which to grow. In late 1991, Sudan presented the perfect opportunity.

Setting the Stage for Terror in Sudan

Dr. Hassan al-Turabi, the Sudanese revolutionary and nominal leader of the country's National Islamic Front (NIF), warmly welcomed Osama upon his arrival in Sudan. Brigadier Omar Hassan Ahmad al-Bashir staged a military coup in 1989, and Turabi was the power behind the throne. He was the most prominent supporter of worldwide terrorism in world history at that time. Turabi openly welcomed terrorists and provided military training and support for groups such as the Hezbollah, Hamas, Palestinian Islamic Jihad, Egyptian Islamic Jihad, and Algeria's Armed Islamic Group. Osama also may have been attracted to Sudan because the new regime followed strict Islamic teachings.

Osama relied on his construction skills to establish himself in Sudan, setting up headquarters in a nine-room complex on El Mek Nimr Street in the capital city of Khartoum. He lived in a three-story al-Qaeda guesthouse in Khartoum's Riyadh City neighborhood. Once there, Osama undertook many projects for the Sudanese government and set up several new companies to build bridges, roads, highways, and airports, among other things. In Sudan, he had a holding company called Wadi al Aqiq, a construction business named Al Hijra, an agricultural company known as al-Themar al-Mubaraka, a trading company called Laden International, and a currency company named Taba Investments. He also owned a leather company, Khartoum Tannery, as well as al-Qaduarat Transport Company, a transportation concern. Osama, however, was not attempting to rebuild his own industrial empire.

While he had incredible business success —at one point he reputedly monopolized several export industries such as sesame and corn products—Osama only formed a means to support the jihad and al-Qaeda. He used his Al-Hijira subsidiary to import explosives, supposedly for construction projects, and al-Qaduarat to move fighters in and out of the country to his al-Mubaraka vegetable farms, which were actually military training camps.

Osama's personal fortune, once estimated between $270 million and $300 million, greatly aided the al-Qaeda organization. Al-Qaeda also reportedly received support through donations from various sources in the Middle East. Saudi-Arabian financial forensics uncovered a group of Islamic clergy who funneled an estimated $50 million in donations to al-Qaeda. The funds were gathered in mosques as alms to Osama.

Al-Qaeda also received funds through the Dubai Islamic Bank, which was controlled by the United Arab Emirates. The covert intelligence community was rife with rumors about Osama's efforts to arm his terrorist army, including purported links to production of chemical VX and the biological agent Ricin. Osama used his companies as fronts to move money and weapons. Al-Qaeda's strength as a terrorist movement in the Middle East continued to grow. Osama contacted an ally of his from the Afghanistan period, Tariq al-Fadhi, and persuaded him to leave semi-retirement in London to head up an al-Qaeda operation in Yemen. Al-Fadhi moved quickly. Within a week of Osama's request, the Yemeni Islamic Jihad formed into a number of active and separate cells. Osama then merged al-Qaeda with Islamic Jihad, the group run by al-Zawahri, and named his personal physician second in command of al-Qaeda, responsible for military operations.

For the Saudi government, Osama's potential as a threat grew monthly. Reportedly, on December 29, 1992, al-Qaeda detonated a bomb in an Aden, Yemen, hotel. Al-Qaeda bombers intended to kill U.S. troops en route to Somalia, but the poorly executed attack failed. The U.S. service people departed prior to the explosion, which killed two Austrian tourists instead. However, Osama reputedly took credit for the al-Qaeda attack, and the Saudi government's level of fear regarding his influence in their kingdom must have mounted. Al-Qaeda had designs on other targets, however.

Americans as Targets

On February 26, 1993, just months after the Yemen bombing, Osama's al-Qaeda followers detonated another large bomb. This time, the bomb blew up in the heart of the U.S. business district, in the parking garage of the World Trade Center. The attack killed six, wounded a thousand others, and caused half-a-billion dollars in damages. It was a tremendous payoff for an estimated al-Qaeda investment of only $3,000 for the bomb materials. Subsequently, authorities captured and found guilty a blind Egyptian cleric, Sheikh Abdel Rahman, and nine members of the *Gamaa Islamiya* terror network. They planned attacks on other targets, including the

Lincoln Tunnel, as well. Rahman entered the United States from Sudan in 1990, despite a history of terrorist activities in his native land. In Sudan, he served time for recruiting members for the Islamic terrorist faction that assassinated Egyptian president Anwar Sadat.

The bomb maker in the garage attack, Abdul Basit Mahmoud Abdul Karim, better known as Ramzi Yousef, trained in Peshawar. To the U.S. intelligence community, assumptions of al-Qaeda influence were obvious and easy to make. Yousef was raised in Kuwait, though his family was Baluch Pakistanis. Educated as an electrical engineer in Wales, Yousef learned to speak English well and had a stellar terrorist career that took him around the world. His attempted terrorism plots included blowing up a dozen or more American passenger jets, assassinating Pope John Paul II, and crashing a plane into CIA headquarters in Langley, Virginia. In Pakistan, Yousef tried to assassinate the first female prime minister, Benazir Bhutto. After the

World Trade Center bombing plot, which he successfully concluded, Yousef fled the United States, but he was captured during an international manhunt. After standing trial, he was convicted.

U.S.-government pressure to curb Osama's group became steady and fierce. In reaction to American pressure, allegedly the Saudi intelligence service unsuccessfully attempted to murder Osama, while he was living in Sudan. Finally, in 1993, realizing Osama's wealth was his greatest protection, the Saudi government decided to freeze all his Saudi assets. Osama was prepared however, and the action didn't stop the al-Qaeda machinery. On October 3, 18 U.S. troops were killed in Mogadishu, Somalia. Again, authorities suspected al-Qaeda-trained terrorists committed the murders. Very publicly, the Saudi government withdrew Osama's citizenship in 1994.

The attacks continued. On November 13, 1995, a car bomb killed five Americans and two Indians outside the American-operated Saudi National Guard training center in Riyadh. Osama commanded more terrorist action, and seven months after the Riyadh bombing, al-Qaeda acted again. On June 25, 1996, a truck bomb detonated outside the Khobar Towers military complex in Dhahran. The bomb killed 19 U.S. servicemen and injured hundreds of others. The Saudi government blamed the attack on Iran or the Iran-backed Shia. In June 2001, the United States indicted 13 members of Saudi Hezbollah—a Shia group with connections to Iran—for the Khobar attack. Nonetheless, U.S. intelligence services continued to take grave interest in Osama, because his jihad against America was underway and unmistakable.

In an interview with American television journalists broadcast in May 1997, Osama explained his reasons for American hatred.

> *The hearts of Muslims are filled with hatred towards the United States of*

America and the American president. The president has a heart that knows no words. A heart that kills hundreds of children definitely knows no words. Our people in the Arabian Peninsula will send him messages with no words because he does not know any words. If there is a message that I may send through you, then it is a message I address to the mothers of the American troops who came here with their military uniforms walking proudly up and down our land … I say that this represents a blatant provocation to over a billion Muslims. To these mothers I say if they are concerned for their sons, then let them object to the American government's policy.

After his denunciation by the Saudi Arabia government, Osama formed the Advice and

Reform Committee (ARC) as a political arm for al-Qaeda to deflect interest in his activities. ARC published several tracts that condemned the Saudi government's apparent reliance on western governments. With international pressure mounting to muzzle Osama in Khartoum, and because ARC was having difficulty communicating with the organization's supporters in Saudi Arabia, Khaled al-Fawwaz became the public face of the council. The ruse didn't work. Osama's profile continued to grow in the Muslim world, and U.S. authorities identified him as a leading activist under the apparent protection of the Sudanese.

On August 23, 1996, Osama confirmed that suspicion, when he announced a call to war against non-Muslims in the Middle East. He authored a tract called the *Declaration of Jihad Against Jews and Crusaders.* Written in Arabic, the newspaper *Al-Quds Al-Arabi* reproduced the tract. The published reports said Osama and his senior associate, al-Zawahri, endorsed a fatwah that bluntly stated Muslims should kill Americans.

> *Our Muslim brothers throughout the world ... Your brothers in the country of the two sacred places and in Palestine request your support. They are asking you to participate with them against their enemies, who are also your enemies—the Israelis and the Americans—by causing them as much harm as can be possibly achieved.*

This enraged U.S. authorities, and bowing to diplomatic pressures, in 1996, the Sudan government finally forced Osama to leave the country. Osama returned to Afghanistan. The United States missed at least two opportunities to seize Osama before he fled Sudan for Afghanistan. Initially, Sudan offered to turn him over, but the United States considered the offer bogus. Instead, the Sudanese reputedly gave Osama three days' notice of the expulsion decision. This provided him enough time to liquidate his assets in Sudan and redirect them to eastern Pakistan.

While Osama was en route to his new headquarters, the United States had a second chance to capture him. His chartered C-130 aircraft, carrying his wives, children, and 150 of his top aides, left Khartoum, but it refueled in the Gulf State of Qatar, a kingdom with friendly relations to America. The United States did not take action.

Once Osama arrived in Pakistan, he no longer feared being captured. He met with senior officers in the Pakistani military, including Mushaf Ali Mir. Allegedly, Mir offered Osama his government's protection if he aligned with the Taliban in Afghanistan. Osama accepted immediately. Mohammad Omar, leader of the Taliban, closely matched Osama ideologically. The ISI helped Osama establish a new headquarters in Afghanistan's Nangarhar province.

In 1999, Osama moved the official headquarters for his terrorist group from Peshawar to Farmihadda, Afghanistan, a few miles south of Jalalabad near the Pakistani border. There, the operation took over a former military base known as Tora Bora, which later became a specific target of U.S. missiles. In the following years, Osama moved the headquarters to a number of different camps in eastern Afghanistan, as he managed to stay one step ahead of his hunters.

Declaration of War

On August 7, 1998, the eighth anniversary of the arrival of American troops in Saudi Arabia, two truck bombs detonated within nine minutes of each other outside the U.S. embassies in Nairobi, Kenya, and Dar es Salaam, Tanzania. Al-Qaeda members referred to the Kenya operation as the *Holy Ka'ba*. The attack killed 212 people—including 12 Americans—and injured more than 5,000 others. The Tanzania attack killed 11 Tanzanians, most of them Muslims. No

Americans died as a result of the Dar es Salaam, Tanzania, attack.

Although the terrorists responsible apparently never received direct instructions from Osama or al-Qaeda, after the Kenya attack, the al-Qaeda distributed a recruiting tape on the Internet. The tape included explicit details about why al-Qaeda detonated the bombs. "It was considered to be the biggest intelligence-gathering center in East Africa," Osama said on the tape. "With the help of God, the hit against it was very strong against the Americans. This is so the Americans can taste something of what we Muslims have tasted."

After al-Qaeda claimed credit for the U.S. embassies bombings in Kenya and Tanzania, U.S. president Bill Clinton issued a top-secret order authorizing the CIA to assassinate the leader of that terrorist cabal. It was in early 1996 that President Clinton signed a CIA finding that Osama threatened U.S. security. The finding established a group made up of a small number of

CIA and FBI agents to build a legal case against Osama and then capture and prosecute him in a U.S. court. The FBI only opened a file on Osama in October 1995.

The U.S. government took its first steps to disrupt al-Qaeda finances in 1998, when it froze $240 million in al-Qaeda and Taliban assets found in U.S. bank accounts after the East-Africa embassy bombings. According to an article that appeared in *The Washington Post*, the U.S. action caused Osama to realize the financial vulnerability of his organization. Apparently, he began immediate moves to transfer his wealth to diamonds and blue tanzanite. Some said Osama relied on the ancient *hawala* underground banking system to move his cash. Prevalent in Pakistan and

TANZANITE

A deep blue gemstone, Tanzanite is found only in a two-square-mile area of Tanzania. Named after its country of origin by the famous New York jeweler, Louis Comfort Tiffany, the $400 million-a-year tanzanite market became a key source of al-Qaeda funding starting in the mid-1990s.

Afghanistan for decades as an interlocking series of money changers, the hawala system's
great advantage was its paperless trail. Clients
made verbal requests to a hawala banker in one
country to deliver cash in another. A handshake
and trust sealed the transaction. Often this
system transferred cash faster than the official
banking systems.

American politicians asked for information about al-Qaeda. They perceived a void in
knowledge, so to rectify this situation, Congress
created the National Commission on Terrorism
in 1998, after the East-Africa bombings.

Terrorism experts asserted the U.S. intelligence community did not have definitive
information describing al-Qaeda until 1999.
Actually, the FBI had such documents as early
as 1996. Briefing memos known as FBI 302s
resulted from interrogations of a man named
Jamal al-Fadl. The FBI did not share this information with politicians.

Al-Fadl was a young Sudanese man who

worked at the Alkifah Refugee Center at the al Farooq mosque in Brooklyn. In 1988, he traveled to Afghanistan and Pakistan and swore bayat to the newly formed al-Qaeda. Osama used al-Fadl as a courier and link to Sudanese intelligence for some time, until in 1996, al-Fadl became greedy. That year, he embezzled $110,000 in illicit commission on the sale of goods from one of Osama's companies. He expected al-Qaeda would seek revenge with his murder and decided to give himself up to U.S. authorities. He became known as Confidential Source 1 (CS-1). The CIA debriefed al-Fadl for six months and then turned him over to the FBI. Al-Fadl provided definitive information on al-Qaeda.

On August 20, 1998, 13 days after the embassy attacks, U.S. President Bill Clinton ordered 80 Tomahawk cruise missiles to strike three al-Qaeda training camps in Afghanistan and the al-Shifa pharmaceutical plant in Khartoum. The first target was a camp complex near the eastern town of Khost. It consisted of six al-Qaeda

bases: al-Badr, al-Badr-2, al-Farooq, Khalid bin
Walid, Abu Jindal and Salman Farsi. Although 20
or so died in the attack, including six of Osama's
followers, the operation failed. Osama and al-
Zawahri left at least 10 days earlier. A bombing
raid by U.S. fighter jets on the pharmaceutical
factory purported to be Osama's weapons manufacturing center destroyed the facility, killing
one and injuring several others. However, the
attack failed, as well. Subsequent investigations of the rubble proved false the allegations
that the factory manufactured chemical weapons. In fact, the company produced 60 to 70
percent of Sudan's pharmaceutical drugs used
to combat deadly diseases including malaria,
tuberculosis, and cholera. The plant offered
vital medicines at 20 percent of world-market
prices. The U.S. government had to pay the
company reparations. The attacks flopped from
the U.S. perspective, but in the Muslim world,
they transformed Osama into a global celebri-
ty. From the Oval Office, Clinton explained his

reasons for the cruise-missile attack. "Our target was terror. Our mission was clear: to strike at the network of radical groups affiliated with and funded by Usama [Osama] bin Laden, perhaps the pre-eminent organizer and financier of international terrorism in the world today," he said.

In February 1998, Osama formed the umbrella framework of the International Islamic Front for Jihad Against Jews and Crusaders. The Islamic Front served as a clearing house and coordinating body for many terrorist groups worldwide. That month, Osama and al-Zawahri arranged for an Arabic newspaper in London to publish, what they called, a fatwah in the name of the Islamic Front. Osama; al-Zawahri, leader of the Egyptian Jihad Group; Rifai Ahmed Taha of the Egyptian Islamic Group; and the leaders of Pakistani and Bangladeshi militant organizations signed *The Declaration of War Against the Americans Occupying the Land of the Two Holy Places.*

On March 12, 1998, a convocation of 40 Afghan *ulema* (clergy) blessed the fatwah. "The Union of Afghanistan's scholars ... declares Jihad according to Islamic law against America and its followers."

At the end of April, Pakistani clerics in Karachi issued a similar fatwah:

> *To kill Americans and their allies, both civil and military, is an individual duty of every Muslim who is able, (in) any country where this is possible, until the Aqsa Mosque (in Jerusalem) and the Haram Mosque (in Mecca) are freed from their grip and until their armies, shattered and broken-winged, depart from all the lands of Islam, (and are) incapable of threatening any Muslim ...*

> *By God's leave we call on every Muslim who believes in God and hopes*

for reward to obey God's command to
kill the Americans and plunder their
possessions where he finds them and
whenever he can.

In May 1998, Osama made another statement entitled *The Nuclear Bomb of Islam*. In that statement, Osama claimed it was Muslims' duty to prepare as much force as possible to attack the enemies of God. He elaborated during an interview in Afghanistan with ABC-TV. He claimed it was more important for Muslims to kill Americans than other infidels.

"It is far better for anyone to kill a single American soldier than to squander his efforts on other activities," he said, advocating for attacks on civilians, as well. "We believe that the worst thieves in the world today and the worst terrorists are the Americans. Nothing could stop you except perhaps retaliation in kind. We do not have to differentiate between military or civilian. As far as we are concerned, they are all targets."

Osama, it seemed, was looking for bigger scores. In the months leading up to 2000, U.S. intelligence agencies suspected as many as 15 plots hatched to kill Americans during New Year's Eve celebrations around the world. However, no one made public statements suggesting that any of those attacks might take place on American soil.

Weeks before the year end, Jordanian security agents intercepted a telephone conversation between an al-Qaeda leader and a suspected terrorist. Zayn al-Abidin Mohammed Husayan, also known as Abu Zubaydah, was born in Saudi Arabia in 1971, but he grew up a Palestinian refugee in the Gaza Strip and had early involvement with *Hamas*. Al-Zawahri's Egyptian terrorist group recruited Zubaydah at age 25, when the group fused with al-Qaeda. Zubaydah was in charge of al-Qaeda's eastern-Afghan camps, and he was responsible for training thousands of Muslim radicals. Jordanian authorities believed Zubaydah, known to be the number three man in the al-Qaeda terrorist organization, cryptically reported on the progress of the plots. They overheard him saying, "the grooms are ready for the big wedding," sending U.S. antiterrorist experts into frenzy. Obviously, al-Qaeda was behind the alleged plans, but no one knew where the strikes would occur.

Millennium Plots

Despite the U.S. special task force, Osama remained untouchable, and his organization became more potent. The telephone call involving Zubaydah late in 1999 indicated al-Qaeda was planning large-scale murder to mark the millennium in American blood. While the U.S. government needed to act preemptively, its options were limited. To stop the terrorists, they first had to find the criminals.

To start, Michael Sheehan, chief of antiterrorism for the State Department made a formal request to the Taliban. The radical Islamic group ruled Afghanistan, and the U.S.

State Department knew it harbored al-Qaeda's operations. Sheehan asked that Osama be turned over to U.S. authorities for prosecution. The request came with a threat. Reportedly, when Sheehan called Wakil Ahmed Muttawakil, the foreign minister of the Taliban, he read a message from President Clinton: "We will hold the Taliban leadership responsible for any attacks against U.S. interests by al-Qaeda or any of its affiliated groups. You will be held personally responsible."

Sheehan likely did not expect the threat to work, and probably only hoped that Taliban pressure on Osama might forestall an attack. As well as Sheehan's call, the state department appealed to friendly governments to initiate sweeps of suspected terrorists.

In Jordan, authorities questioned 13 previously arrested, suspected terrorists. A search through one of the suspect's homes uncovered plans for constructing bombs, along with details about al-Qaeda camps in Afghanistan.

From confessions obtained during interrogations authorities learned one of the "weddings" was to have been a truck bomb sent to destroy the Radisson SAS Hotel in Amman, Jordan. Other plans included murdering American tourists in machine-gun crossfire at sites such as the Temple of Hercules in Amman.

CHAPTER 4

Homeland Security

For months after the September 11, 2001, attacks, U.S. warplanes flew nonstop combat air patrols over several key cities, including Washington, D.C., and New York. Prior to March 2002, when such missions were reduced, navy and air force fighter aircraft flew more than 19,000 combat air patrols. The flights cost more than $500 million.

Americans still didn't feel safe. Almost

3000 victims of the World Trade Center attack, the disruption of the U.S. transportation infrastructure, and the negative affect on the American economy had taken a toll on every citizen. Americans demanded action to protect the nation from future attacks.

On September 20, 2001, Bush announced the establishment of the Office of Homeland Security at the White House, as well as the appointment of Pennsylvania governor Tom Ridge as homeland security advisor. Ridge's mission was "to develop and coordinate the implementation of a comprehensive national strategy to secure the United States from terrorist threats or attacks."

As Ridge worked, so did al-Qaeda. In April 2002, an al-Qaeda-suspected bomb exploded in a Tunisian synagogue, killing 16 people. In July, another al-Qaeda-suspected bomb blew up outside the U.S. embassy in Karachi and killed 11. In October, a bomb in a Bali nightclub in Indonesia killed 202 and was linked to Riduan

Ismuddin, also known as Hambali—an Indonesian cleric with suspected al-Qaeda links.

By November 2002, antiterrorism sentiment was at a fever pitch in the United States. The Department of Homeland Security (DHS) was put in place as an outcome of Bush's initiative. U.S. Congress approved the DHS, consolidating eight other cabinet departments and merging 170,000 employees from 22 agencies.

In his announcement signing the Homeland Security Act into law, Bush said: "Today, we are taking historic action to defend the United States and protect our citizens against the dangers of a new era."

He said the new department would analyze threats, guard borders and airports, protect critical infrastructure, and coordinate the response to future emergencies.

> *We recognize our greatest security is found in the relentless pursuit of these cold-blooded killers. Yet, because*

terrorists are targeting America, the front of the new war is here in America. Our life changed and changed in dramatic fashion on September the 11th, 2001.

In the last 14 months, every level of our government has taken steps to be better prepared against a terrorist attack. We understand the nature of the enemy. We understand they hate us because of what we love. We're doing everything we can to enhance security at our airports and power plants and border crossings. We've deployed detection equipment to look for weapons of mass destruction. We've given law enforcement better tools to detect and disrupt terrorist cells which might be hiding in our own country.

Bush outlined five expected outcomes of the act. First, the newly formed DHS could analyze intelligence information on terror threats collected by the CIA, the FBI, the National Security Agency and others. "The department will match this intelligence against the nation's vulnerabilities—and work with other agencies, and the private sector, and state and local governments to harden America's defenses against terror."

BIOSURVEILLANCE

The Bush-administration's *BioWatch* program protects over 30 U.S. cities by continually monitoring the air for biological agents potentially released in a bioterror attack by air. The program reportedly costs around $80 million a year to run.

Second, the DHS would gather and focus efforts on the challenge of cyberterrorism, as well as the danger of nuclear, chemical, and biological terrorism.

Third, state and local governments would have one federal domestic security agency to turn to in the case of emergency. At the time, more than 20 agencies divided those responsibilities.

Fourth, the new department would bring

together the agencies responsible for border, coastline, and transportation security.

Finally, the department would work with state and local officials to prepare the U.S. response to any potential future terrorist attack. "We have found that the first hours and even the first minutes after the attack can be crucial in saving lives, and our first responders need the carefully planned and drilled strategies that will make their work effective."

As a result of the Homeland Security Act, the DHS's *Information Analysis and Infrastructure Protection (IAIP) Directorate* was responsible for coordinating the protection of the nation's critical infrastructure. Today, the IAIP coordinates infrastructure protection activities across federal agencies and directs resources and efforts to reduce the vulnerability of U.S. infrastructure to terrorism.

In 2004, IAIP focused on identifying key assets, determining vulnerabilities, performing risk analysis, and implementing protective measures. In 2005, IAIP continued to identify and map critical assets. Cybersecurity was a key element of that infrastructure protection. In 2005, IAIP also launched a biosurveillance initiative to improve surveillance and the federal government's capability to identify a bioterrorist attack. Within IAIP, the Science and Technology (S&T) Directorate expanded monitoring and improved the analysis tools used to detect and respond to possible attacks.

Barely two years after DHS's creation, however, the department underwent a massive reorganization. When Michael Chertoff took control of the DHS in February 2005, he ordered a management review of the department , which, by then, had 183,000 employees. The shake-up drew upon the United States Department of Defense's organizational model in an attempt to create joint leadership at the top of the department with the objective to better synchronize security efforts.

"If there was one disappointment I had

as I walked out the door," former Deputy Secretary of Homeland Security, Admiral James M. Loy, was quoted as saying, "it was that we weren't as far as we could have or should have been in protecting the core infrastructure of the nation."

With the reorganization, the DHS created a new intelligence office to connect the information the department received from state and local authorities with what it learned from U.S. intelligence agencies. The department also focussed on emergency preparedness. The United States aimed to achieve the same swift and practiced response demonstrated by the British after the London bombings. As part of Chertoff's redesign, a segment of the Federal Emergency Management Agency (FEMA) became a part of a new division that focused on preparedness.

Containing the Container Bottleneck

Securing the U.S. border and transportation systems continues to be an enormous challenge for the DHS. Ports of entry into the United States from Canada and Mexico stretch across 7,500 miles (12,000 km) of land. Each year, the border processes more than 500 million people, 130 million motor vehicles, 2.5 million railcars, and 5.7 million cargo containers. On an average day, the ports of Los Angeles and Long Beach, California, offload 18,000 containers. For authorities to inspect every offloaded container, it would take 270,000 people hours per day, an obviously impossible target for inspectors. Complicating matters is the fact that trucks ship containers arriving on the east and west coasts of the United States as "in bond" to their destination and can take up to 30 days to receive a customs inspection.

Maritime trade represents 2 billion tons of freight—worth more than $1 trillion—and the figures are projected to double by the year 2020. Each year, U.S. ports process 3.3 billion barrels of imported oil and 5 million cruise ship passengers. These same waterways handle 110,000 commercial fishing vessels and 134 million ferry passengers. With 95 percent of all U.S. overseas trade passing through 361 American ports, port security has become a top priority for the DHS.

As a solution to the dilemma, the Container Security Initiative (CSI) prescreens cargo before it reaches American shores. The first phase of CSI focused on implementing the program at the top 20 foreign ports, which ship approximately two-thirds of the containers to the United States. Phase two expanded the program to additional ports based on volume, location, and strategic concerns, including shipping radioactive materials.

In June 2005, DHS secretary Michael Chertoff announced that the ports of Los Angeles and Long Beach would have complete Radiation Portal Monitor (RPM) coverage by year's end. He said that by December 2005, all international container traffic and vehicles exiting the facility would be screened for nuclear materials or hidden sources of radiation by a total of

90 RPMs. RPM systems do not emit radiation but can detect it emanating from nuclear devices, dirty bombs, special nuclear materials, natural sources, and isotopes commonly used in medicine and industry.

Protecting the Homeland in Canada

Though al-Qaeda leader Osama bin Laden declared Canada a "legitimate target" in March 2004, it is the only country on his list yet to be attacked.

One of Tom Ridge's earliest actions as Bush's homeland security advisor, was a meeting with Canada's minister of foreign affairs, John Manley. On December 12, 2001, the two men signed the Smart Border Declaration, with a 30-point action plan to speed and secure the flow of people and goods between the United States and Canada, while tightening border security into the United States.

Canadian authorities did not believe the border was as "leaky" as Americans claimed. Canada established its own civilian spy network on July 16, 1984, which the Canadian government believed controlled the matter of terrorism in Canada. Canada created the Canadian Security Intelligence Service (CSIS) when the Royal Canadian Mounted Police Security Service disbanded, recognizing the differences between security intelligence activity and law enforcement. The CSIS spied on any individuals who threatened national security. They were a force of highly trained operatives without weapons, closely scrutinized by the Canadian parliament. The CSIS did not have law enforcement powers.

At first, the CSIS's resources countered the spy activities of foreign governments in Canada, but in response to the rise of terrorism worldwide, the CSIS devoted a large proportion of its resources to counterterrorism. The CSIS Act strictly controlled the ways that the CSIS collected information and who may view the information. For example, the CSIS can gather information only about those individuals or organizations suspected of engaging in espionage; sabotage; activities directed, controlled, financed, or otherwise significantly affected by a foreign state or organization; and those involved in acts of political violence or terrorism on Canadian soil.

U.S. politicians felt uneasy about the international perception that Canada was an immigrant-friendly place. The myriad ethnic backgrounds of Canada's populace made it a perfect destination for would-be terrorists, according to the FBI. Quebec and Ontario, and in particular the city of Toronto, were hotbeds of potential terrorist threat. Approximately 61 percent of Canada's estimated 750,000 Muslims resided in Ontario. Five percent of those Muslims lived in Toronto—the city with the highest Muslim population in North America. American security experts wanted tighter border scrutiny to prohibit Muslims from traveling south, including special identification cards and biometric records.

By April 2005, Canada had spent $9.3 billion on various security programs, tightened its controls over processing applications for travel documents used by visitors to the country, and had taken steps to implement international security standards at Canadian ports. Canada also implemented a vessel-tracking system and radar technology in maritime surveillance.

In July, the Canada Border Services Agency (CBSA) made two announcements concerning border security issues. The CBSA announced that it employed more than 12,000 agents, and it would add 270 more over the next five years. In addition, the government added a new security system to several airports. Called CANPASS Air, the service uses iris identification to speed pre-approved travelers through border clearance. However, travelers are not required to participate in CANPASS Air. Canadians must pay a $50 membership that is valid for one year. The minister of public safety and emergency preparedness, Anne McLellan, was among the first

to try the new biometric identification system
at the Edmonton, Alberta, airport. The service
also was made available in Calgary, Halifax,
Montreal, Toronto, Vancouver, and Winnipeg. It
would soon be established in Ottawa, as well.

CHAPTER 5

The Future

Western intelligence agencies and governments realize that the "war on terrorism" is one that will never end. As extremists of one type are stymied, their organizations morph, like viruses immune to antibiotics. Al-Qaeda, though severely curtailed by the war in Afghanistan, is a hydra with many heads. This was evidenced by the London Tube bombings, which appear to have been conducted by a previously unknown group of terrorists acting without direction from Osama and his co-commanders.

America's job, it seems, is to secure its safety internally and restrict access to unwanted terrorists. However, according to U.S. politicians, there are many holes to fill in policy, organization, and procedures.

Too Few on the Borders

On April 20, 2005, Senator Judd Gregg, the chairman of the subcommittee of the United States Senate Committee on Appropriations, claimed, "… our borders aren't effective anymore … We have virtually no security along our borders; people are pouring over the borders illegally. It has gotten so bad that in Arizona, citizen groups are now seeking to enforce the borders. The electronic surveillance capability along the border is nonexistent right now from all I can tell. There's been a total breakdown in the camera structures, and the unmanned vehicle program has basically been stopped, even though it was proving very successful."

Senator Robert Byrd (D-WV) echoed Gregg's remarks at the same hearings. "In fiscal year 2004, Immigration and Customs Enforcement removed a record 150,000 illegal aliens from this country. However, we know that more than 10 million illegal aliens reside in this country. Two-and-a-half million illegal aliens have overstayed their tourist or work visas," he said. "There are 370,000 illegal aliens who have knowingly disobeyed orders to leave the country. Immigration and Customs Enforcement teams deported 11,000 of them in 2004, but more than 35,000 others were added to the list. The system is not working."

The Nuclear Threat

Weapons of mass destruction pose the most nightmarish scenario for American intelligence agencies fighting to quash terrorist attacks in the United States. Osama unequivocally stated such weapons are suitable for the jihad. "We don't consider it a crime if we tried to have nuclear, chemical, biological weapons," he was quoted as saying.

There is no evidence publicly available that shows al-Qaeda has the capabilities of using weapons of mass destruction; although, inquiries made by hijacker Mohamed Atta about purchasing crop-dusting planes in Florida in early 2001 indicate chemical or biological warfare is on the terrorist agenda. It is certainly possible that al-Qaeda has acquired rudimentary nuclear materials. Testimony by Ressam indicated he witnessed terrorists test cyanide gas as a weapon in the al-Qaeda training camps. The World Trade Center garage-bombing trial also supports the contention that al-Qaeda can use chemicals to gas their victims. Osama has funds to purchase materials, such as nuclear waste, and likely has tried to do so.

For antiterrorism organizations, one of the largest future concerns is the possible use of toxins to create plagues or infect a large population. The technology and knowledge exists for well-funded and highly motivated terrorist groups to mount such an attack. Although the list of potential agents is long, only a handful of pathogens, including anthrax, smallpox, bubonic plague, botulinum toxin, hemorrhagic fever viruses, and tularemia, could paralyze a large city or region. In the future, antiterrorism authorities must prepare to fend off this dynamic threat list of biological pathogens that are also bioterrorism weapons.

Terrorism Timeline

May 1, 1961
First U.S. aircraft is hijacked.

April 18, 1983
Sixty-three people are killed and 120 are injured in a 400-pound (180 kg) suicide truck-bomb attack on the U.S. embassy in Beirut, Lebanon. The Islamic Jihad claims responsibility.

October 23, 1983
Suicide truck-bomb attacks are made on American and French military compounds in Beirut, Lebanon. A 12,000-pound (5,400 kg) bomb destroys the U.S. compound, killing 242 Americans, while 58 French troops are killed when a device destroys a French base. The Islamic Jihad claims responsibility.

June 14, 1985

Two Lebanese Hezbollah terrorists hijack a Trans-World Airlines flight en route to Rome from Athens. The eight crew members and 145 passengers are held for 17 days, during which time, one American hostage is murdered.

June 23, 1985

An Air India Boeing 747 is destroyed over the Atlantic, killing all 329 people aboard. Both Sikh and Kashmiri terrorists are blamed for the attack.

December 21, 1988

Pan American Airlines Flight 103 is blown up over Lockerbie, Scotland. All 259 people on board are killed.

1988   Osama bin Laden establishes al-Qaeda (the Base).

April 1991

Saudi Arabia expels Osama bin Laden, who takes up residence in Sudan.

February 26, 1993
> The World Trade Center in New York City is badly damaged when a car bomb planted by Islamic terrorists explodes in an underground garage. The bomb leaves six people dead and 1,000 injured.

April 9, 1994
> Saudi Arabia strips Osama bin Laden of his citizenship.

March 20, 1995
> Twelve people are killed and 5,700 are injured in a sarin nerve-gas attack on a crowded subway station in the center of Tokyo, Japan. A similar attack occurs nearly simultaneously in the Yokohama subway system. The Aum Shinrikyo cult is blamed for the attacks.

April 19, 1995
> Right-wing extremists Timothy McVeigh and Terry Nichols destroy the Federal Building in

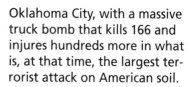

Oklahoma City, with a massive truck bomb that kills 166 and injures hundreds more in what is, at that time, the largest terrorist attack on American soil.

Early 1996

The CIA sets up a special unit to track Osama bin Laden's activities. Sudan offers to turn over Osama to the United States or Saudi Arabia. Both refuse the offer.

May 18, 1996

Sudan expels Osama bin Laden, who moves to Afghanistan.

June 25, 1996

A fuel truck carrying a bomb explodes outside the U.S. military's Khobar Towers housing facility in Dhahran, killing 19 U.S. military personnel and wounding 515 persons, including 240 U.S. personnel. Several groups claim responsibility for the attack.

January 8, 1998

Ramzi Yousef is sentenced to life without parole for orchestrating the 1993 World Trade Center bombing.

February 22, 1998

Osama bin Laden issues fatwah, calling for attacks on American citizens.

August 7, 1998

A bomb explodes at the rear entrance of the U.S. embassy in Nairobi, Kenya, killing 291. Approximately 5,000 are injured. Almost simultaneously, a bomb detonates outside the U.S. embassy in Dar es Salaam, Tanzania, killing 10.

August 20, 1998

U.S. cruise missiles strike suspected terrorist installations in Afghanistan and Sudan.

October 12, 2000
> Two suicide bombers attack the U.S.S. *Cole*, killing 17 people.

September 11, 2001
> The World Trade Center is attacked with commercial airliners.

September 27, 2001
> President Bush unveils a new plan to enhance aviation safety and security.

October 7, 2001
> U.S. and British forces launch attacks on Afghanistan.

October 9, 2001
> Al-Qaeda spokesperson, Sulaiman Abu Ghaith, issues a statement calling for a holy war against the United States.

October 14, 2001
> President Bush recommends that Congress allocate $1.5 billion to the Department of

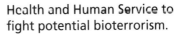

Health and Human Service to
fight potential bioterrorism.

October 18, 2001
Each of four terrorists linked
to Osama bin Laden are
sentenced to life in prison in
connection with the 1998 U.S.-
embassy bombings in Kenya
and Tanzania.

October 26, 2001
President Bush signs the
Patriot Act, a broad-based
antiterrorism bill.

November 7, 2001
Osama bin Laden tells a
Pakistani journalist that he
possesses nuclear and chemical
weapons.

November 19, 2001
President Bush signs an
aviation safety bill and
says, "The law I sign should
give all Americans greater
confidence when they fly."

December 13, 2001

The Pentagon releases a videotape of Osama bin Laden bragging about the September 11 attacks. "We calculated in advance the number of casualties ... We calculated that the floors that would be hit would be three or four floors. I was the most optimistic of them all."

December 22, 2001

British citizen Richard Reid attempts to detonate explosives hidden in his shoes on an American Airlines flight from Paris, France, to Miami, Florida.

February 4, 2002

President Bush unveils his $2.1 trillion budget—doubling spending for homeland security and allotting $38 billion for increased border security and financial support for local law enforcement agencies.

March 12, 2002
>The director of homeland security, Tom Ridge, announces the Homeland Security Advisory System, which classifies terrorist threats using a graduated color-scale and provides a response framework for federal, state, and local governments.

March 20, 2002
>A car bomb explodes outside the U.S. embassy in Lima, Peru, killing nine people.

April 11, 2002
>A blast outside a synagogue in Djerba, Tunisia, kills at least 16 people.

April 13, 2002
>Spanish police arrest Ahmed Brahim, who is believed to be the chief financial officer of the al-Qaeda network.

April 19, 2002
>The FBI releases a public warning that 1,200 banks in the

northeastern United States may be targets for terrorist attacks. The warning is based in part on information received from Abu Zubaydah, a high-ranking al-Qaeda officer in U.S. custody.

May 15, 2002

The New York Times reports that an FBI agent wrote a memo the previous summer urging an investigation of Middle-Eastern men who had enrolled in flight schools in the United States. The memo mentioned that the men might use the flight lessons to perpetrate acts of terrorism.

June 22, 2002

Canadian police arrest terror suspect Adel Tobbichi, who is accused of providing forged passports and of helping to plan a terrorist attack against the U. S. embassy in Paris, France. Police begin investigating possible links between Tobbichi and al-Qaeda.

July 17, 2002

The report on *Counterterror ism Intelligence Capabilities and Performance Prior to September 11* highlights critical failures of the U.S. intelligence community. It contends that the FBI, the CIA, and the NSA were stymied by poor interagency cooperation and an inability to use new technologies.

July 26, 2002

The U.S. House of Representatives approves legislation creating a Homeland Security Department.

October 12, 2002

A bomb attack kills 202 people at a Bali, Indonesia, nightclub. On March 2, 2005, an Indonesian court finds Muslim cleric Abu Bakar Ba'asyir guilty of conspiracy and sentences him to 2½ years in prison.

November 28, 2002
> Fifteen people die in a bombing at an Israeli-owned hotel in Mombassa, Kenya.

May 2003
> Al-Qaeda suicide bombs explode in Riyadh, Saudi Arabia, in Znamenskoye, Chechnya, and in Casablanca, Morocco, killing at least 130.

August 5, 2003
> A car bomb kills 10 and injures 150 others at the J.W. Marriott Hotel in Jakarta, Indonesia.

November 8, 2003
> A bombing at a housing complex a few miles from Riyadh's diplomatic quarters kills at least 17 people.

November 2003
> Attacks on a synagogue in Istanbul, Turkey, kill 25 people. Later in the month, two bombings in the city target the British consulate and the HSBC Bank.

March 11, 2004
> Explosives hidden in backpacks explode in a Madrid train station, killing 191 people

April 21, 2004
> Attacks in downtown Riyadh, Saudi Arabia, kill 10 people.

December 6, 2004
> An attack on the U.S. consulate in Jeddah, Saudi Arabia, kills five staff and leaves four militants dead. The Saudi wing of al-Qaeda claims responsibility.

July 2005
> Four bombs explode July 7 in the London transport system, killing 56 and injuring 700 people. More explosions occur on July 21, but no one is killed.

August 18, 2005
> Saleh Mohammed al-Aoofi, al-Qaeda's top leader in Saudi Arabia, is killed by police in Medina.

Glossary

Allah: Arabic word for God

Bedouins: Arabic desert-dwelling nomads

caliphate or kalifate: the political embodiment of Islamic rule; successors to the Prophet Mohammed held the title "caliph."

emir: the political leader of an Islamic community

fatwah: a legal ruling issued by an Islamic scholar

hajj: the Muslim pilgrimage to the holy city of Mecca, which all Muslims—men and women—with sufficient resources are urged to perform once during their lifetime. Men who have performed the *hajj* may take the title of *al-haj*; women *al-haja*.

Hezbollah: Party of God, formed in Iran by the Ayatollah Khomeini

Islam: a religion based on submission or surrender to God's will, as revealed to Mohammed

Islamism: the ideological belief in the requirement to enact the political tenets of Islam as the basis of political life

jihad: struggle in the defense of Islam

Koran (Quran): the Muslim holy book, believed to contain the revelations conveyed to Mohammed from God through the archangel Gabriel in the seventh century

kufr: term used to describe that which is not Islamic

mujahideen: fighters in a jihad or holy war; individuals may also be referred to as *jihadis*

Shariah: the Islamic way or path; a code of law based on the Koran

Sufism: the Islamic mystic movement; practices that center on devotion to earlier Muslims who were renowned for their piety and, in some cases, their supernatural powers, called *baraka* in Arabic

Sunnism and Shiism: the two schools of Islam ulema: the body of learned Islamic advisors empowered to pronounce religious rulings

umma: the global community of Muslims, which transcends nationality and nation-states and links all Muslims into a single community

Wahhabi: a member of a Muslim sect founded by Muhammad ibn Abd al-Wahhabi in the 1700s which is dominant in Saudi Arabia. It is an austere form of Islam that preaches a literal interpretation of the Koran.

Amazing Facts and Figures

Types of international terrorist attacks against Americans by percentage, 1998–2001

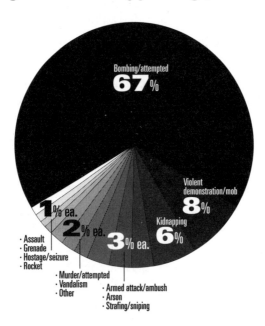

Bombing/attempted
67%

Violent demonstration/mob
8%

Kidnapping
6%

1% ea.
· Assault
· Grenade
· Hostage/seizure
· Rocket

2% ea.
· Murder/attempted
· Vandalism
· Other

3% ea.
· Armed attack/ambush
· Arson
· Strafing/sniping

Source: Political Violence Against Americans, 1987 through 2001. *Office of Intelligence and Threat Analysis, Bureau of Diplomatic Security, Department of State.*

Total international terrorist attacks, 1998–2001

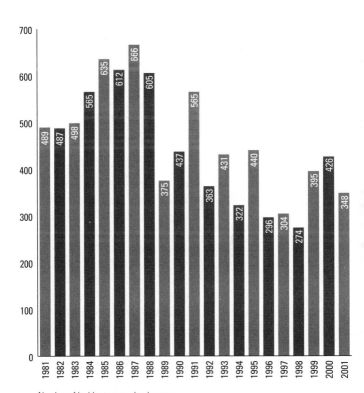

Number of incidents per calendar year

Source: U.S. Deptartment of State

U.S. Nuclear Power Plants Safe from Attack?

Nuclear-power critics claim that despite the DHS's stepped up caution, much work needs to be done before the plants are safe from terrorist attack. Currently 103 nuclear power plants supply 20 percent of America's electricity. As well, 37 smaller research reactors are located at universities and other organizations in the U.S. Allegedly, nearly half of the plants that underwent Nuclear Regulatory Commission (NRC) security drills in the past decade—33 of 68—failed and showed significant security weaknesses. A real terrorist attack could result in partial or complete meltdown of the reactor cores. In 14 of the pseudo attacks, radiation could have been released to the atmosphere. On its website, the Nuclear Energy Institute (NEI), a nuclear industry trade association, stated that, "reinforced concrete containment structures ... have been designed to withstand the impact of hurricanes, tornados, floods, and airborne objects up to a certain force. Design requirements with respect to aircraft impacts are specific to each facility." In other words, the safety of a specific nuclear plant targeted by such an airplane attack is debatable.

Sources: U.S. Nuclear Regulatory Commission, Congressional Research Service Reports

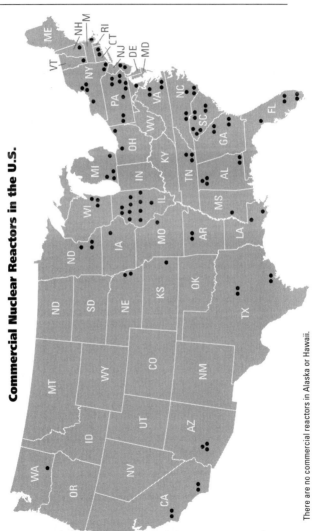

Commercial Nuclear Reactors in the U.S.

There are no commercial reactors in Alaska or Hawaii.

Past preferred terrorist targets

Target	Injuries	Fatalities
Abortion clinics	2	2
Airports and airlines	2,360	2,359
Business	9,709	4,932
Diplomatic	8,405	1,273
Educational institutions	1,311	459
Food or water supply	5	0
Government	7,160	3,366
Journalists and media	221	179
Maritime related	263	130
Military	4,360	1,451
Non-gov't. organizations	256	284
Other	2,177	1,406
Police	4,569	2,722
Private citizens	13,814	5,675
Religious figures	4,834	1,648
Telecommunication	73	35
Terrorists	513	402
Tourists	1,473	583
Transportation	11,688	1,936
Unknown	900	309
Utilities	336	196
Total	**74,429**	**29,347**

Source: Oklahoma City-based Memorial Institute for the Prevention of Terrorism. Figures recorded since 1968.

Possible new preferred targets

1	Transportation infrastructure (airports, trains)
2	Financial businesses (banks)
3	Diplomatic locations such as consulates
4	Government buildings
5	Military installations (barracks)
6	Religious institutions (churches and mosques)
7	Universities
8	Agriculture (crops, herds)
9	Utilities (water and power)
10	FBI facilities, political conventions
11	Cyberterrorism of computer networks
12	Sea ports
13	Chemical plants

Capabilities of different sizes of car bomb

Vehicle description	Maximum air blast range	Lethal air blast range	Minimum evacuation distance	Falling glass hazard
Compact sedan	500 lbs (227 kg)	100 ft (30 m)	1,500 ft (457 m)	1,250 ft (381 m)
Full-size sedan	1,000 lbs (455 kg)	125 ft (38 m)	1,750 ft (534 m)	1,750 ft (534 m)
Passenger/cargo van	4,000 lbs (1,818 kg)	200 ft (61 m)	2,750 ft (838 m)	2,750 ft (838 m)
Small box van	10,000 lbs (4,545 kg)	300 ft (91 m)	3,750 ft (1,143 m)	3,750 ft (1,143 m)
Box van, water/fuel truck	30,000 lbs (13,636 kg)	450 ft (137 m)	6,500 ft (1,982 m)	6,500 ft (1,982 m)
Semi-trailer	60,000 lbs (27,273 kg)	600 ft (183 m)	7,000 ft (2,134 m)	7,000 ft (2,134 m)

Source: Bureau of Alcohol, Tobacco and Firearms

ANTHRAX FACTS

• The amount of anthrax needed to cause widespread infection is not easily accessible, and the few centers that have the organism on hand are closely monitored.

• To become infected with the virus, anthrax spores must make contact with a break in the skin or be inhaled directly.

• Anthrax is not contagious.

• Generally, anthrax cannot be contracted from eating food or water, but poorly cooked meat from infected livestock can transmit the infection.

• Introducing sufficient anthrax into water supplies is highly unlikely due to increased security measures.

• After inhaling anthrax spores, a person may experience flu-like illness that progresses to severe breathing difficulty, weakness, and muscle aches. If anthrax is contracted through contact with a skin break, infection usually begins as a small, swollen bump at the site of contact. This swells and ulcerates over time. If anthrax is ingested, it causes abdominal pain, abdominal swelling, and bloody diarrhea.

• Incubation times range from one to eight days. If a person has been exposed to anthrax, however, he or she should seek medical assistance immediately. Anthrax can rapidly cause life-threatening illness.

• People can be vaccinated against anthrax, but given the low level of risk to the general populace and limited vaccine supplies, governments likely will not undertake large-scale immunization.

• Anthrax is sensitive to commonly available antibiotics.

What Others Say

"Islamic governments have never and will never be established through peaceful solutions and cooperative councils. They are established as they (always) have been. By pen and gun. By word and bullet. By tongue and teeth."

al-Qaeda training manual

"Terrorist attacks can shake the foundations of our biggest buildings, but they cannot touch the foundation of America. These acts shatter steel, but they cannot dent the steel of American resolve."

George W. Bush

"If the American Airlines jet that traveled down the Hudson Valley en route to the Twin Towers had instead banked a left turn into one of Indian Point's twin reactors, the resulting disaster would have been even more horrific than the World Trade Center catastrophe."

Robert F. Kennedy, Jr.

"Response to these threats must not be discriminatory. They can be eliminated only through comprehensive countermeasures undertaken on the basis of the principles and norms of international law against all those who use terror to achieve their goals, leaving them no hope of escaping unpunished. Nothing can justify terrorism. There should be no room for double standards and narrow national interests."

Vilayat Guliyev, minister of foreign affairs, Azerbaijan

"In security parlance, they are hardened targets. They [nuclear power plants] are not going to be the ones terrorists go after because [a successful attack] would be too difficult."

Mitch Singer, Nuclear Energy Institute

"The terrible thing about terrorism is that ultimately it destroys those who practise it. Slowly but surely, as they try to extinguish life in others, the light within them dies."

Terry Waite, British religious adviser, hostage in Lebanon

"I think America has no experience with terrorism or even with war. In Europe, we know a little bit more about these things."

Bono, front man for the band U2 and political activist

"It's very rare that even the smallest window is opened on the inner workings of Canadian intelligence services and when it is, it's for a darn good reason. At the present time, I think the disclosure is appropriate because it should signal to all of Canada we're global leaders and we've got it under as much control as we can muster. It also should be a perceived warning to people who want to dabble in terrorist violence in Canada. They may be daily facing one-way intelligence mirrors."

Richard Kurland, Vancouver lawyer and policy analyst

"The prospects of a future attack on the U.S. are almost a certainty. It could happen tomorrow, it could happen next week, it could happen next year, but they will keep trying. And we have to be prepared."

Vice President Cheney on Fox News Sunday, May 19, 2002

"The horrific events of September 11
remind us that we must continue to work
with other nations to confront terrorism
and ensure the full force of Canadian
law is brought to bear against those who
support, plan, and carry out acts of terror
—we will cut off their money, find them
and punish them."

*Anne McLellan (then Canadian
Minister of Justice)*

"Americans think bin Laden should die.
But not just an ordinary execution. I
wouldn't be surprised if they hung him
upside down and beat him to death."

Yoshio Horita, Japanese journalist

"You can't beat your enemy anymore
through wars; instead you create an
entire generation of people revenge-
seeking. These days it only matters who's
in charge. Right now that's us—for a
while at least. Our opponents are going
to resort to car bombs and suicide attacks
because they have no other way to win.
... I believe [Donald Rumsfeld, U.S.
Secretary of Defense] thinks this
is a war that can be won, but there is
no such thing anymore. We can't beat
anyone anymore."

George Clooney, actor

"Make no mistake about it:
We are at war now—with
somebody—and we will stay
at war with that mysterious
enemy for the rest of our lives."

Hunter S. Thompson,
journalist and author

"I think one has to say it's not just simply a matter of capturing people and holding them accountable, but removing the sanctuaries, removing the support systems, ending states who sponsor terrorism. And that's why it has to be a broad and sustained campaign."

Paul Wolfowitz, U.S. Deputy Secretary of Defense

"It's important ... that those engaged in terrorism realize that our determination to defend our values and our way of life is greater than their determination to cause death and destruction to innocent people in a desire to impose extremism on the world."

Tony Blair, British prime minister

Bibliography

Aburish, Said K. *The House of Saud.* St. Martin's Griffen: New York, 1996.

Bergen, Peter L. Holy War, Inc. *Inside the Secret World of Osama bin Laden.* The Free Press: New York, 2001.

"Bin Laden verses honor Cole attack." *Reuters Newswire* reprinted in *The Seattle Times* March 2, 2001.

Blanche, Ed. "The Egyptians Around Bin Laden." *Jane's Intelligence Review.* December 2001.

Bodansky, Yossef. *Bin Laden: The Man Who Declared War On America.* Forum, an imprint of Prima Publishing: Roseville, CA, 1999.

Corbin, Jan. *Al-Qaeda: In Search of the Terror Network That Threatens the World.* Thunder's Mouth Press/Nation Books: New York, 2002.

Douglas, Farah. "Report Says Africans Harbored Al-Qaeda: Terror Assets Hidden in Gem-Buying Spree." *The Washington Post* December 29, 2002.

Dyer, Joel. *Harvest of Rage—Why Oklahoma City Is Only the Beginning*. Westview Press, a division of HarperCollins Publishers: Boulder, CO, 1997.

Flynn, Stephen. *America the Vulnerable—How Our Government Is Failing to Protect Us From Terrorism*. HarperCollins Publishers: New York, 2004.

"Fraser targets antiterror spending." *Canadian Press* Monday April 4, 2005.

Gertz, Bill. *Breakdown—How America's Intelligence Failures Led to September 11*. Regnery Publishing, Inc.: Washington, D.C., 2002.

Gold, Dore. *Hatred's Kingdom: How Saudi Arabia Supports the New Global Terrorism*. Regnery Publishing, Inc: Washington, D.C., 2003.

Hoge, James F. Jr. and Gideon Rose (editors). *How did this happen? Terrorism and the new war*. Perseus Books Group: New York, 2001.

Husband, Mark. *Warriors of the Prophet: The Struggle for Islam*. Westview Press: Boulder, CO, 1998.

Ismail, Jamal. "I Am Not Afraid of Death." *Newsweek International* January 11, 1999.

Lake, Anthony. *Nightmares*. Little, Brown and Company: Boston, 2000.

Lance, Peter. *Cover Up: What the government is still hiding about the war on terror*. Regan Gooks: New York, 2002.

Ledeen, Michael A. *The War Against the Terror Masters*. Truman Talley Books: St. Martin's Press, New York, 2002.

Netanyahu, Benjamin. *Fighting Terrorism: How Democracies Can Defeat Domestic and International Terrorism*. Farrar Straus Giroux: New York, 1995.

Parenti , Michael. *The Terrorism Trap: September 11 and Beyond*. City Lights Books: San Francisco, 2002.

Posner, Gerald. *Why America Slept: The Failure to Prevent 9/11*. Random House: New York, 2003.

Randal, Jonathan. *Osama: The Making of a Terrorist*. Alfred A. Knopf: New York, 2004.

Robinson, Adam. *Bin Laden Behind the Mask of the Terrorist*. Arcade Publishing: New York, 2002.

"The 9/11 Commission Report." W.W. Norton & Company: New York, 2003.

"U.S. Missed Three Chances to Seize Bin Laden." *Sunday Times of London,* An Insight Team Investigation, January 6, 2001.

Wheeler, Jill C. *Tuesday, September 11, 2001: The Day That Changed America.* ABDO Publishing Company: Edina, Minnesota, 2002.

Wheeler, Yonah and Michael S. Swetnam. *Usama bin Laden's al-Qaeda: Profile of a Terrorist Network.* Transnational Publishers: Ardsley, NY, 2001.

Wright, Robin. *Sacred Rage: The Wrath of Militant Islam.* Simon & Shuster: New York, 1985.

Photo Credits